NATURAL ORDERS

EMAIL MARKETING AUTOMATION
STRATEGY for SMALL
ONLINE BUSINESS

Copyright © 2022 Matt Treacey

All rights reserved. No part of this book may be reproduced in any form or by any electronic or mechanical means, including information storage and retrieval systems, without permission in writing from the publisher, except by reviewers, who may quote brief passages in a review.

ISBN: 978-0-6455074-1-6

Cover design by Jason Anscomb
Creative Commons image credits: LucasMartinFrey, Yuri Gurevich, Chrmichel, Torsten Pursche.
"Hooked Model" image used by permission of Nir Eyal.

Sydney, Australia.
Visit symbiosgrowthautomation.com

NATURAL ORDERS

EMAIL MARKETING AUTOMATION
STRATEGY for SMALL
ONLINE BUSINESS

MATT TREACEY

CONTENTS

INTRODUCTION viii

NATURAL ORDERS 1
  The Top-Down Cascade 3
  Mimicking Nature 5
  The Stages Of Succession 10
  Summary 17

THE WALLED GARDENS 19
  The Bottom-Up Cascade 21
  I. Platform Risk 22
  The Walled Gardens 28
  Aggregation: How Walled Gardens Grow 30
  Ii. ...Or, Optimism 36
  How To Cultivate A Walled Garden 38
  Traffic To Subscriber Conversion 43
  Summary 52

I. DISPERSAL 55
  Engagement: Solving The Top-Down Cascade 60
  The Five Awareness States 67
  The Curation Advantage 71
  The Awareness Automation 75
  Segmentation And Personalization 87
  Summary 88

II. RECRUITMENT 91
- Personalization 95
- The Black Box Problem 96
- The Semantic Layer 99
- A Tag Taxonomy 101
- The Semantic Automation 104
- Putting It All Together 119
- Summary 122

III. ESTABLISHMENT 125
- The Constraints To Growth 132
- Traffic, Conversion, Lifetime Value 134
- Lifetime Value Automation 145
- New Channel Opportunities 161
- Summary 163

CONCLUSION 164
- Seeing The Forest For The Trees 168

REFERENCES 174

ACKNOWLEDGEMENTS 183

DOWNLOAD FREE RESOURCES

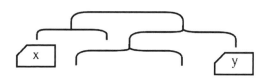

To access a free tag taxonomy planning document, as well as the other free resources that come with this book, please visit: symbiosgrowthautomation.com/natural-orders-resources

INTRODUCTION

We ought to be thankful to nature
for having made those things which are necessary easy to be discovered;
while other things that are difficult to be known are not necessary.

Epicurus

More than two-thousand years strong, the advice of Epicurus remains relevant today. At first, it reads self-evident: do the obvious thing. The next step is usually right in front of us.

But there's a subtlety here that's easily overlooked. Sometimes, *we discover too late* we didn't do something that turned out to be necessary.

We order more stock with the expectation our sales trend will continue, only for a shock event to flatten it overnight. We post on social media only to discover the external link we included has been penalized by the algorithm. A global pandemic hits and we realize we should have had more of the essentials.

It's happened to all of us. In every case, retrospect is always 20/20. There are plenty of names for when it happens: a black swan, a "tail risk" event, or just plain old bad luck. The cause is always the same: we failed to adequately prepare; we neglected to put in place the measures to avert disaster.

Necessary Discoveries

If you're reading this book, you're likely considering the best way to use email marketing and automation in your business.

You may already be aware of some of the ways it can help you. Some of the stats about the channel are widely known: that email contacts the largest and most active group of internet users, some ~3.9 billion individuals, each spending on average 2–3 hours a day in their inboxes.[1] Or, that it's also the most highly engaged audience online, with average email open rates around double the equivalent expected engagement of an average social media post.[2]

---

[1] Convinceandconvert.com. 13 Email Marketing Statistics That Are Shaping 2019 and Beyond [ONLINE] Available at: https://www.convinceandconvert.com/digital-marketing/email-marketing-statistics/

[2] Sendgrid.com. 2019 Email Benchmark and Engagement Study - SendGrid [ONLINE] Available at: https://sendgrid.com/resource/2019-email-benchmark-and-engagement-study/

Maybe you've heard about email's great ROI: with a return on average around ~$51 USD for every dollar spent. When used correctly, the ROI from email dwarfs any alternative, with strategies such as paid search typically yielding in comparison just $2 for every $1 spent.[3]

This "used correctly" is key. Email marketing must be implemented properly in order to reveal its more advanced benefits. High ROI and engagement are great on their own, but what makes email special goes beyond these basic propositions. Used correctly, email allows direct communication with your market, enabling you to collect and compound your customer data, as well as the endless possibilities of automation.

Knowing just some of this potential is enough to pique the interest of most small online business owners. Less known are the risks. They seem almost under-discussed in comparison. Yet anyone with experience of email marketing automation will immediately know what I'm referring to.

Small business owners new to email marketing often find themselves with their revenue suddenly halved, their engagement dwindling to nothing, and their hard-won subscribers shuffling away in quiet exodus. After nearly a decade building email automation for small online businesses, I've learned that these types of catastrophes can be grouped into two forms: the *Top-Down Cascade* and the *Bottom-Up Cascade*.

---

[3] Dma.org.uk. Email's ROI increases, despite concerns about testing and GDPR | DMA [ONLINE] Available at: https://dma.org.uk/press-release/emails-roi-increases-despite-concerns-about-testing-and-gdpr

The Top-Down Cascade	The Bottom-Up Cascade
The top-down cascade is the consequence of poor foundations. Your email list collapses in on itself.	In the bottom-up cascade, the foundations don't collapse, but are simply pulled out from under you.
It begins with a drop in the amount of people interacting with your emails. After not too long they start unsubscribing from your emails *en masse*.	Maybe you're banned from the platform you depend on for traffic. Or maybe there was an algorithm change that now penalizes the reach of your posts.
Similar to a collapsing ecosystem, your database begins slowly dying.	In every case, access to your audience is taken away without recourse; your business no longer has legs to stand on.

The lessons of both cascades are the same – we need a strategy when it comes to email marketing and automation. It's the only way to make sure you aren't exposing yourself to the common risks of the top-down and bottom-up cascades.

Perhaps more importantly, we also need a strategy to make sure you're able to access the more sophisticated benefits of email marketing we touched on above. Think about your current email marketing strategy:

- Are you building goodwill with your subscribers so they stick around long term?
- Are you actively collecting data about them so you can personalize their emails?
- Are you waking every morning to new sales from automations?
- Do you have any automation set up at all?

If this doesn't describe your situation you don't need to feel you're missing out. The truth is, most small online businesses aren't doing any of these things. And when you look at the state of things, it's easy to understand why. There are countless individual blog posts, courses and one-off tactics out there for the channel. But there are few comprehensive systems that actually take those elements and place them into a broader context.

As the cascades above illustrate, the key to a successful email marketing strategy is much more than a sum of independent parts. There are no comprehensive guides out there telling you how to go from beginner to advanced. No blog post will give you insight for how precisely this channel should sit in your broader marketing mix, or how it can uniquely help your business.

This book intends to solve that gap. Over the next two chapters, I'll start by outlining why and how we can address these bottom-up and top-down cascades. In doing so, we'll set the proper foundations which will allow you to reap the many unique benefits email marketing automation has to offer.

Epicurus in his wisdom was right. The necessary things are always discovered in the end - all too easily, whether we like it or not. This book is your guide to avoid discovering those necessary things too late.

NATURAL ORDERS

All I could do was watch everything fall apart. With each passing week our emails were reaching less of our subscribers. Our engagement was cooked. The amount of people leaving our email list would soon outpace the rate we could replace them. Our "unsubscribes" were spiraling out of control.

What was happening? As head of growth, it was on me to come up with an answer. Maybe this was just the expected drop off rate as our email list was growing? Maybe we'd "exhausted" our list by sending too many offers?

But it wasn't any of these. We had a healthy list. We never sent spam. Up to this point, everything had been running perfectly.

If you're new to email and automation, the truth is, things can go south pretty quickly. Often, like I was, you can only watch on helplessly as your list disintegrates in front of you.

Unsubscribes and low engagement, as I experienced early in my career, are bad enough in isolation. What makes it worse is when you don't know *why* it's happening.

But what causes this? How can something as simple as sending a few emails so often end in disaster? I'd later realize that what we were experiencing was something I now refer to as the "top-down cascade".

The Top-Down Cascade

The top-down cascade typically looks like this:

- **You start off with a set of simple components.** Single campaigns, a small list of subscribers, the ability to add tags and fields to these subscribers and send emails in automations.

  But after some time adding new campaigns and building automations these simple elements compound. Soon, there's a spider-web of interrelationships. Before you know it, you've lost the full picture of how it all fits together.

- **This results in outsized effects**. With everything becoming more connected over time, little things can begin to have far-reaching consequences.

  One small detail can be overlooked in an automation and hundreds of subscribers are removed from the database. Or a seemingly insignificant element is ignored in a subscriber segment and your campaign is sent to the completely wrong audience.

- **Further impacting this are *feedback loops*.** Effects seemingly begin to compound on themselves.

  Once your open rates start falling, it becomes harder to reverse the process. Once people start unsubscribing it becomes even more likely that you will lose more in the future. You soon realize these types of self-compounding effects become a defining feature of your email automation setup.

This combination of compounding simplicity, nonlinear effects, and feedback loops are the hallmark traits of advanced email marketing automation. These same traits just so happen to be precisely what Professor Paul Cilliers lists as defining features of complexity in his 2000 paper "What can we learn from a theory of complexity?".[4,5]

While it definitely isn't rocket science, setting up email marketing automation *does* possess a certain level of complexity. Look inside any reasonably sophisticated email marketing software (EMS) account, and you'll find several automated sequences, with dozens of interconnected components and processes running simultaneously.

At a certain point with email and automation, we seem to cross a bridge. We go from simply sending emails, to managing a system with dozens of interacting components.

This isn't a bad thing in itself - it only becomes a problem when we fail to recognize we've arrived at that point. When we are unaware the above processes are taking place we expose ourselves to the risks of the top-down cascade.

As things become more complex, they can more easily get out of hand:

- Without intentionally designing our feedback loops, we become subject to the ones that naturally arise, which may or may not be in our best interest.

- In ignoring the potential for outsized effects, we fail to look holistically at our decisions or apply the necessary attention to detail to avoid these effects.

- Perhaps most common of all, when trying to design a masterpiece automation system from scratch, we fail to use simple building blocks that avoid things getting away from us too quickly.

---

[4] Journal.emergentpublications.com. What can we learn from a theory of complexity? – Emergence: Complexity and Organization [ONLINE] Available at: https://journal.emergentpublications.com/article/what-can-we-learn-from-a-theory-of-complexity/

[5] Eolss.net. General Features of Complex Systems [ONLINE] Available at: https://www.eolss.net/Sample-Chapters/C15/E1-29-01-00.pdf

Mimicking Nature

The first time I came across the top-down cascade, I didn't understand what was happening. After a frustrating few weeks thinking it through, the answer came from an unlikely place. I realized what was happening to our email list was actually something I was already familiar with.

After obtaining the relevant degree in my early twenties, I worked briefly as an Ecologist with the Australian Government. Half a decade studying taxonomy, population dynamics, plus time in the field for study and work had given me an understanding of how natural systems work.

When I experienced the top-down cascade for myself, there weren't really any adequate terms in marketing or business to describe what had happened. On the other hand, the concepts and analogies for the same process I'd studied and observed in Ecology proved extremely helpful.

We're all familiar with the idea of an "ecosystem collapse". Whether via oil spill or bulldozer, we know how nature falls apart when we stress the system to its limits. Just like those collapses, a similar "cascade" seemed to be happening in our email database. Just like a collapsing ecosystem, our list was slowly dying.

All the factors were there. We had a replacement rate (churn), mortalities (unsubscribes) and fecundity (rate of new entrants). Just like an ecosystem, there was an overall health that needed to be managed. Just like an ecosystem, something had gone wrong at the foundations.

I saw that in order to avoid the top-down cascade, looking to nature's solutions may be our best bet. After all, the classic "complex system" is nature itself. The best examples of Cillier's hallmark traits of compounding simplicity, non-linear effects and feedback loops are best found in the forests, oceans and gardens that surround us every day.

Mine wasn't an original conclusion. You don't have to look far to see just how often nature is cited as the genesis for innovation.

While walking his dog in the Alps, Swiss engineer George de Mestral famously conceived the idea for Velcro. Noticing the way burrs would stick to his pet's fur, he came up with the concept for the now widely known hook-and-loop fastener, patented in 1955.[6,7]

Another example is the bullet train. When Japanese engineers found that regular-shaped trains produced dangerous sonic booms entering tunnels at high speeds they sought an alternative design. Looking to nature, the engineers turned to the beak of the Kingfisher as inspiration. The characteristic bullet train shape we see today not only solved the sonic boom issue, but reduced electricity usage and allowed even higher speeds of travel due to being more aerodynamic.[8]

This natural inspiration isn't a recent practice. Even centuries earlier, Leonardo da Vinci's studies on the flight of birds led to his schematics of an early flying machine he dubbed the "Ornithopter". In contemporary times, the University of London looks again to birds to further improve the mechanics of flight. Mimicking the peregrine falcon, the world's fastest flying bird, researchers have developed 3D-printed polymer filaments designed after the falcon's wing-tip feathers, improving safety and preventing engine stalling.[9,10]

This design approach, today often referred to as "Biomimicry", was organized into a formal structure in 2006 to promote the approach. Today, the Biomimicry Institute's "Ask Nature" online resource

---

[6] Velcro.co.uk. Who Invented VELCRO® Brand Fasteners? | VELCRO® Brand [ONLINE] Available at: https://www.velcro.co.uk/about-us/history/

[7] Asknature.org. Versatile Fastener Inspired by Burrs — Innovation — AskNature [ONLINE] Available at: https://asknature.org/innovation/versatile-fastener-inspired-by-burrs/

[8] Asknature.org. High Speed Train Inspired by the Kingfisher — Innovation — AskNature [ONLINE] Available at: https://asknature.org/innovation/high-speed-train-inspired-by-the-kingfisher/

[9] The Australian, (2020). How the World's Fastest Bird Will Make the Aircraft of the Future [ONLINE] Available at: https://www.theaustralian.com.au/nation/defence/how-worlds-fastest-bird-will-make-the-aircraft-of-the-future-safer/news-story/24c0b0e43b72c241a518fd30fcbb66a9

[10] Howitworksdaily.com. Nature inspired aircraft [ONLINE] Available at: https://www.howitworksdaily.com/the-peregrine-falcon-inspired-aircraft/

documents hundreds of case studies where nature has been cited as the genesis to solutions for complex design and engineering challenges.[11]

The popularity of the discipline grows yearly, nearly matching the number of elegant solutions it's yielded. Centuries later, it seems da Vinci's convictions were correct, in that "… *human subtlety will never devise an invention more beautiful, more simple or more direct than does nature because in her inventions nothing is lacking, and nothing is superfluous*".[12]

In searching for solutions to our problems we often try to reinvent the wheel, but the most elegant design solutions are right around us all the time. They're stress-tested and perfected by billions of years of evolution and countless generations of trial and error, yielding solutions perfectly fit for their environment. The biomimetic approach recognizes this and seeks to simply observe what solutions are already present in the natural world.

Yet for all its virtues this approach has been somewhat overlooked in marketing and business. This is surprising, as there are likely parallels to be drawn between the most effective growth systems we see in business and the spectacularly successful growth systems that surround us every day in the natural world.

Why haven't we looked more toward nature to inform the way we grow our businesses? After all, the sole function of marketing is growth. Where better to imitate nature than in the design of a system intended, from its basic purpose, for growth?

Rory Sutherland, Creative Director at advertising agency Ogilvy, reflected on this oversight in his 2019 book "Alchemy", writing *"My analogy between signalling in the biological world and advertising in the commercial world may explain something I have noticed for years: if you talk to economists, they tend to hate advertising and barely understand it at all, while if you talk to biologists they understand it perfectly"*.[13]

---

[11] Asknature.org. Innovation Inspired by Nature — AskNature [ONLINE] Available at: https://asknature.org/
[12] Richter, I. A. et al. (2008) Notebooks. Cary, NC: Oxford University Press.
[13] Sutherland, R. (2019) Alchemy: The dark art and curious science of creating magic in brands, business, and life. New York, NY: HarperAudio.

Ogilvy's observation hits the right notes, but the broader idea of the "market as an ecosystem" yields plenty of other parallels:

- Similar to Sutherland's observation, the "selective trait" of an organism seems to be equivalent to a product's "unique selling point". Whether in nature or the market, there needs to be some unique exploit to improve the chances of survival.

- Whether talking about nature or marketing, a "niche" always refers to a competitive strategy used by a product or an organism.

- When we speak of a "total addressable market" for a new business venture, this seems to be similar to working out the "carrying capacity" of an ecosystem. The implications are the same – there is a maximum limit of market entrants or organisms that can be sustained.

- In ecology we also delineate between types of market participants. We refer to "keystone" or "foundation" species – important organisms critical to forming entirely new habitats. There is an overlap here with businesses which create entirely new markets such as Amazon, Uber or Airbnb.

There are many other parallels. Admittedly, some of these analogies are somewhat superficial. But it was these connections that eventually led me to consider how this model might apply *specifically* in an email marketing context.

I began looking at the problem more and more through the lens of *the email list as an ecosystem*. If this were true, what would it mean for improving the overall health of the list? What would it mean for attracting new subscribers? How could we best mimic the growth patterns we find in nature?

There was clear value in this model for helping to solve the problems I was encountering every day with my work. Yet I wasn't prepared for just how valuable it would become.

Email Marketing Automation, Designed for Growth

It was through this lens that I was able to solve the problem of the top-down cascade. I had already come to the conclusion that there was something wrong with the foundations of our email list. As we'll later explore, I discovered that those foundations were poor *engagement* and *retention*.

Once I had figured out exactly what those foundations needed to be, everything became easier. Once we found solutions to improve these two factors, the top-down cascade became a non-issue.

Since then, where other marketers have seemed to fall into many of the pitfalls and dangers of the channel, I've been able to sidestep them. I could actually avoid this all-too-common scenario of a deluge of unsubscribes and a downward spiral of engagement.

But I was able to do much more than simply avoid these risks. I soon discovered that laying this foundation at the beginning was the key to getting the most out of the channel.

While I initially started applying principles from ecosystems to avoid outcomes like the top-down cascade, in truth the biggest benefits came as something of a side-effect. In copying nature to avoid catastrophe, I also found a highly effective system for *growth* in general.

After implementing various forms of *Natural Orders* for almost a decade, I've seen how powerful this system can be as an email marketing automation strategy. I've seen it used to usher in dozens of new products to market, double revenue for a business over the space of a year, and even launch a new seven-figure venture. As of writing, various forms of the *Natural Orders* system are generating millions of dollars in sales for small online businesses across the USA, the UK and Oceania.

I'm now convinced that progressing an email list's *development,* just as we would see in the natural world, is the best way to achieve the greatest profitability and most robust security over the long-term. Again, it was a concept from ecology that proved more useful than anything I could find in business and marketing.

The Stages of Succession

By mimicking the stages of development of an ecosystem, we use the proven patterns of growth in nature to avoid the common causes of collapse and failure that surprise so many new to the channel. In doing this, we build an email marketing strategy designed from the beginning for continual growth.

Ecologists refer to these natural ecosystem progressions as the "Stages of Succession".[14] At its most basic point, an ecosystem starts with bare rock. Soon, fungi and microorganisms anchor in the cracks to form the first layer. As these proliferate, they break down the rock to form soil.

I. This soil forms a basic structure, inviting more microorganisms, producing more nutrients, and even hosting our first simple plants, such as grasses.

II. This increases the capacity of the soil further. More plants. Eventually small shrubs and bushes from nearby environments can send their seeds to take hold and flourish.

III. With this new diversity, capacity increases again. Trees begin to grow. A canopy layer forms, then an understorey, and over time a rainforest hosting countless animals and natural processes.

Credit: Lucas Martin Frey

---

[14] Clements, F. (1916) "Plant Succession: An Analysis of the Development of Vegetation," Carnegie Institution of Washington, 242.

The Stages of Succession are well studied, and it's known that only by progressing first through the early stages can the later stages be reached. It's not possible to go straight from rocks to rainforest.

Just like Cillier's complex systems, this strategy specifically addresses the mechanisms underlying the top-down cascade:

- Intentionally designing our own *feedback loops* will avoid them manifesting in ways that work to our detriment. By basing our strategy on strong engagement, retention and conversion, we can make sure our system has feedback loops which lead to more growth, instead of collapse.

- The strategy has *non-linear effects* built in. But instead of these creating outsized impacts that result in confused subscribers and mass unsubscribes, we'll tap into the patterns in your email database that help you identify your most profitable top customers.

- Crucially, the system itself is very *simple*. It's just three stages, with three respective goals. Just as in nature, we start with a simple process that repeats to compound into something greater.

- Finally, the system is *adaptable*. After making sure the simple structure is in place, you can then customize the system so it works best for you. Being designed for growth from the start, the ability to scale easily is built in.

On that last point, it's this in-built ability to grow and scale that ultimately compelled me to write this book. Let's take a look at exactly how *Natural Orders* can take your email marketing automation strategy, and the growth of your business, to the next level.

Stage I — Dispersal

Stage I. Dispersal: How to Build a Risk-Free Business

The first stage – *Dispersal* – is where we build our email list foundations. Just like an ecosystem, we need to make sure we're creating an environment where new entrants not only visit but want to stick around. We do this by ensuring that we always deliver value with every email we send.

Doing so solves the top-down cascade. You won't have to worry about your subscribers leaving *en masse*, or your engagement slowly dwindling to nothing. You also won't have to worry about having access to your market taken away from you - the "bottom-up" cascade we'll cover in the next chapter.

Building these strong foundations isn't just essential, it also opens you to the other benefits that come with a risk-free business. By building a healthy and engaged email list, you'll create an asset that can increase your valuation, and allows you to take offers direct-to-market with an audience you actually own and control. With a healthy email list comes an on-demand traffic source you can direct anywhere online, influencing social media algorithms, creating partnerships, and freeing you from the whims of the almighty algorithm.

Stage II — Recruitment

Stage II. Recruitment: More Time, More Leverage

With Stage I complete, engagement and retention are at a high baseline. The *Recruitment* stage is where we then focus on maximizing *conversions*. Looking at our email list again as an ecosystem, only a certain number of entrants will reside there permanently, or "establish". Similarly, there will be many subscribers joining our email list, but only a percentage of those will purchase our products or services. By understanding the factors influencing that outcome, we can systematically improve conversions and revenue.

To do this, we'll build automations that collect data revealing more about our customer avatar and their journey to purchase. With this data, we'll have the knowledge of how to best segment your audience, which allows us to send highly *personalized* offers. This superior timing and relevance is by far the best method to improve *conversions*.

Setting up the recruitment stage gives you your first glimpses of what it's like to have an automated system generate sales for you, 24 hours a day, seven days a week. It also grants you the ability to create a truly "data-driven" marketing strategy, beyond just a simple buzzword. Not only will the data we're collecting about our customers help improve conversions, it will allow you to define metrics and KPIs that tie back to goals, which can increase the accountability of team members assigned responsibility to those numbers.

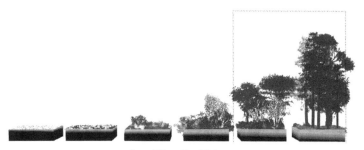
Stage III — Establishment

Stage III. Establishment: More Revenue, More Freedom

The system we've built by this point will now be able to reveal and exploit new revenue opportunities that couldn't possibly have been known previously. With a surfeit of data, healthy foundations and regular sales, we'll finally be in a position to make more strategic marketing decisions.

Just like in an ecosystem, there are certain individuals that produce outsized effects. The most successful businesses in the world, just like the most productive ecosystems, are the ones that can leverage the largest possible returns from these key individuals.

In *Establishment*, we'll leverage the patterns of growth shared between both natural systems and your email database to identify your top customers, and double down on them with advanced automations. The strategies in this chapter are designed to optimize revenue and finally realize the full potential of what email marketing and automation have to offer.

We Must Cultivate Our Garden

The table below shows an overview of the Natural Orders system, the goals of each stage, how we'll achieve them, and the automations we'll build. Over the course of the following chapters, you'll gain an understanding of the broader purpose of each stage, and how they work in unison to develop your subscribers into customers.

Among all the satisfactions that come from working for yourself, there's really nothing that beats waking to find that the system you've built has generated new sales. Admittedly, this idea of building a business that sells by itself is something of a search for the golden fleece. Yet it was what began my fascination with marketing automation, and by extension, email.

When properly used, we can in fact get quite close to what seems like an impossible goal. The system works on its own, it generates sales, and it can definitely take your business to the next level. But it's the perspective shift that comes with this pursuit that is truly valuable. In fact, it can be one of the most transformative of your business life.

STAGE	FOUNDATION	DISPERSAL	RECRUITMENT	ESTABLISHMENT
GOAL	TSC	Engagement	Conversion	Lifetime Value
METHOD	Improve Optin Placements	Provide Value Progress Awareness	Personalization	Increase New Orders Increase Repeat Orders Increase Average Order Value
AUTOMATIONS	N/A	Awareness Automation	Semantic Automation	LTV Automation

Overview of the Natural Orders System

Investing in email and automation is the easiest step you can take from working *in* your business, to working *on* your business. The automations we'll build with *Natural Orders* will help you decouple your time from your income. This alone should be worth the time investment.

But before we can get started, it's important to understand a slightly broader context. It's important to see the full context of where email marketing sits in relation to other digital marketing channels and the unique advantages it affords small online business owners. Without this, it's impossible to appreciate its full importance, or the best way to consider its use for maximum impact.

In the Introduction, I mentioned there were two types of cascades small online business owners often face. While the *top-down cascade* is what happens when everything falls in on itself, this is solved by the automation built in the Dispersal stage. But there is another cascade we need to address.

The *bottom-up cascade* is what happens when your business is pulled from beneath your feet. In the next chapter, The Walled Gardens, we'll cover what this is, why this exists, and how to avoid it. In doing so, the full picture of how to get the most out of email marketing and automation will be complete.

Summary

- **The Top-Down Cascade** is a common way many new to email marketing automation become unstuck. Unsubscribes, poor engagement and deliverability become issues that get in the way of getting the results they want.

- After running into this issue myself early in my career, I found that my background as an Ecologist helped me to see the **parallels between the email database and a simple ecosystem**.

- By progressing the growth of your email marketing system like a natural ecosystem, you can avoid the common forms of collapses common to the channel.

- It turns out that mimicking nature in this way not only avoids collapse, **but produces growth**, as I've seen with dozens of businesses I've worked with.

- **The Natural Orders system** is the best way to build a profitable, robust email marketing automation strategy for a small online business.

A sprung tree (*Tetrameles nudiflora*) grows from the ruins of Ta Prohm Temple. Siem Reap, Cambodia

THE
WALLED GARDENS

For 28 year old eCommerce store owner Hayley, it's been self-evident that *what's necessary is easily discovered.*

Hayley runs an eCommerce store selling potted house plants. Most of her website visitors arrive from her popular Instagram account where she posts to promote her products. She's scaled quickly from her humble beginnings of a few posts selling plants from a small inner-city apartment.

Building her business, one thing has flowed naturally from the other. When the plants are wilting she waters them; when a post performs well on Instagram, followers increase. When followers increase, she sells more plants. Do the obvious thing, and the next steps always reveal themselves.

She's avoided what's unnecessary and built a thriving business because of it. She no longer has the stresses and expectations of her previous job - she sets her own hours, doesn't have to deal with any office politics, and even makes more money. She works on her own terms, with the freedom of time and flexibility in her day that she's always wanted.

Yet Hayley is to discover her own Epicurean lifestyle will soon reveal the subtleties of its maxims. One day Hayley wakes to find Instagram has released a new update. The release notes state there have been some changes intended to limit hate speech on their platform. She notices this new update has affected her account. For some reason, the algorithm has begun to penalize pictures of her plants.

Overnight, the amount of likes and comments Hayley would typically see on a new post have halved. She attracts less followers, gets less traffic to her site, and in turn sells less plants. Her revenue takes a hit. It turns out Instagram's updates aren't yet a perfect science.

Scrambling and anxious, Hayley reaches someone in customer support, but all they can tell her is that they're sorry for her loss. She realizes she's powerless against the changes made by Instagram. After all, was it really likely a multi-billion dollar company with millions of users was going to be able to help her specific case? It's not like they're going to waste their developers' time patching a new update all due to the sufferings of the owner of a single account.

But for Hayley, the situation is serious. Taking advantage of the location-independent nature of her business, she's long since moved out of her small inner-city apartment into a three-bedroom house in the country. With few job opportunities around her, she's at a loss for how she'll make up the lost profits and meet her newly acquired mortgage repayments.

If a giant question mark over where she'll live isn't stressful enough, Hayley also has a garage full of plants she's ordered to service her previous sales trend. With orders halved and with no power to reclaim them, all she can do is watch as her stock slowly wilts away with her losses.

Quite literally overnight, Hayley's new lifestyle has collapsed beneath her feet. She's gone from optimistic about the prospects of her growing business, to facing losses on her product order and possibly having to sell her home, while anxiously looking for any kind of work she can find to try to stay afloat.

The Bottom-Up Cascade

Retrospect is always 20/20. Everything seemed fine, until it was too late. Hayley gave up her job, time and energy to pursue this business. These basic sacrifices have always been part of the contract undertaking any new venture. But the risks she was ultimately exposed to went beyond this.

Without knowing it at the time, Hayley was exposing herself to the bottom-up cascade. As Hayley now realizes, her large Instagram account was a great traffic source, but ultimately, it wasn't hers. In reality, she spent two years as a contracted employee for Instagram, with her page providing value and experiences to their users, and in the end gaining no benefit for herself. She was tending to a garden that wasn't her own; a vassal on borrowed land.

The worst part is that Hayley has nothing to show for her efforts over the past two years. Her customers were all coming from Instagram. Now they've disappeared, her business has gone with them. She has no assets besides a website that's no longer receiving any traffic. She couldn't sell her business if she tried.

Hayley's story is becoming an increasingly common one. Every year it's becoming more risky to operate a small business on the internet. Imagine waking one morning to find your ability to communicate with your market has been taken away; that you have zero influence over your ability to access your customers from one week to the next; that you are subject to sudden rule changes that strip you from all future profit, with zero recourse.

These anxieties are simply a realized awareness of the bottom-up cascade. What makes it so insidious is that it's so rarely spoken of. Yet simply addressing and understanding it, we can make more informed decisions about how to mitigate it.

I. Platform Risk

What Hayley experienced has been referred to as "Platform Risk" - the risk associated with building a business reliant on a third-party. The ubiquity of stories like Hayley's has led to this becoming an everyday term for many small online business owners and tech-industry commentators.[15,16,17,18]

But the ills of platform risk were presaged. Tim Wu's 2011 book *The Master Switch: The Rise and Fall of Information Empires* was prophetic of the decade that followed.

---

[15] Eugenewei.com. "Platform" risk — Remains of the Day [ONLINE] Available at: https://www.eugenewei.com/blog/2015/3/14/platform-risk

[16] Stevefaktor.com. The Risk that Ate the Digital Entrepreneur - Surviving Platform Risk [ONLINE] Available at: https://stevefaktor.com/platform-risk-devours-digital-entrepreneurs/

[17] Druriley.com. Platform Risk - Dru Riley [ONLINE] Available at: https://druriley.com/platform-risk/

[18] Blog.simeonov.com. Startup anti-pattern: platform risk | HighContrast [ONLINE] Available at: https://blog.simeonov.com/2013/03/05/platform-risk-anti-pattern/

Examining information technologies spanning innovations from radio, to telephone, TV and the internet, Wu reveals a common thread between each. Each of these transformative technologies underwent a similar pattern of development: beginning with idealistic notions by their inventors; invariably followed by widespread competition as they first achieved market adoption; and then eventual monopolization by powerful, typically existing, institutions.

The FM radio band was one such technology. Developed by an idealistic inventor with hopes of becoming a powerful and open new communications technology, it eventually saw keen commercial interest from existing power brokers once its advantages became apparent. Litigations, policy changes and ruthless competition from incumbents on the existing AM band, as Wu writes, *"quietly campaigned to relegate FM radio to irrelevancy"*.

As would be the case for many innovations to come, the once transformative potential of the FM band was blunted as it was eventually absorbed into an existing monopoly.

The development of TV followed a similar path. After the opening of the first TV broadcasting station in 1928, the years that followed saw existing players from the radio industry enter the fray (those same powers that devoured the nascent FM band), followed by fierce competition, regulations and lawsuits. The result was, as with all these technologies, an eventual "comfortable duopoly" occupied by just two networks.

Looking back into history, it's apparent there's a trend for all new information technology innovations to follow a similar pattern. Wu goes on to give further examples of subsequent innovations, from cable TV to the internet, in what he terms "… *the Kronos effect: an effort by an existing media power to devour a suspected challenger in its infancy*".

Writing in 2022, it seems the Kronos effect might actually possess some level of mythic truth. The internet has, so far, charted a similar path over its 35 years as the technologies that came before it. Beginning with open-source protocols maintained by idealistic non-profit groups, the internet's development could originally be defined by a counterculture ethos; its early days having notions of it becoming the ultimate means of connection and expression between individuals.

These services now provide billions of people from all corners of the world access to powerful and often free-to-access technology. But it hasn't arrived without problems. Today, the individuals for whom the internet was originally intended now face conflicts with the tech corporations who enabled its now global scale. The early idealism has gradually receded, with the majority of its services now operated by large tech corporations, many born from the same Bay-area counterculture of its inventors.

The individuals who today choose to build on these platforms find themselves increasingly subject to definitive and often arbitrary rule changes by the controlling corporations.

Without a firm understanding that access to our audiences often lies entirely in the hands of these platforms, we gamble building on shaky foundations, over-reliant and over-exposed to the policies and decisions of an entity that, ultimately, doesn't put our interests first.

Small online business owners must now be vigilant in assessing potential exposures to platform risk. And it isn't just limited to Instagram. From diminishing returns for post visibility on Facebook, cut-throat business practices affecting marketplace sellers on Amazon, or the ever-shifting goal posts of the development of Google's search algorithm, history has so far yielded plenty of examples.

Facebook

Not long after the release of Wu's book, the then emerging issue of declining post visibility on Facebook became apparent to those who had built large audiences using the social media giant's service. In a 2012 article for the Observer titled "*Broken on Purpose: Why Getting It Wrong Pays More Than Getting It Right*",[19] author and entrepreneur Ryan Holiday was among the first to draw attention to the company's throttling of its audience-builders in a high-profile publication.

---

[19] Observer.com. Broken on Purpose: Why Getting It Wrong Pays More Than Getting It Right | Observer [ONLINE] Available at: https://observer.com/2012/09/broken-on-purpose/

Businesses who had depended on access to audiences they had built on Facebook were now being told they must pay to reach them. The result of these changes was outrage from those who had already made large investments into doing so. In the opening lines of the article, Holiday takes aim: *"It's no conspiracy. Facebook acknowledged it as recently as last week: messages now reach, on average, just 15 percent of an account's fans. In a wonderful coincidence, Facebook has rolled out a solution for this problem: Pay them for better access"*.

Under the false premise of a fair and open channel to connect and build an audience, the slow throttling of post visibility seemed to some as dishonest. In another 2012 article, online entrepreneur Jason Sadler complained of the changes: *"We were lured to Facebook under the pretense that we would be offered a free service to connect with other people. I'm just not a fan of changing the rules half-way through the game"*. [20]

Unfortunately, many have had to learn the hard way that for these platforms, these sorts of tactics are the game itself. As one 2013 news article on the issue of Facebook's declining post visibility struck the warning bell: *"you are not in control — Facebook is"*.[21]

But the risks associated with relying on a third-party platform for access to your market isn't unique to Facebook. As it's come to become a controlling interest in online retail, Amazon have also developed practices not always in the interests of their small business partners.

Amazon

As of 2021, Amazon took home ~51% of online retail spending that year, representing 9.2% of all US retail.[22] As the platform grows and

---

[20] Jason Sadler. It's Not Cool That Facebook Wants Me to Pay To Reach My Fans With Promoted Posts - WSJ [ONLINE] Available at: https://www.wsj.com/articles/SB10001424052702303740704577521072755665762

[21] Mathew Ingram. Remember, Facebook isn't a platform for you to use - you are a platform for Facebook to use - Gigaom [ONLINE] Available at: https://gigaom.com/2013/03/04/remember-facebook-isnt-a-platform-for-you-to-use-you-are-a-platform-for-facebook-to-use/

[22] Pymnts.com. Amazon, Walmart Nearly Tied In Share Of Retail | PYMNTS.com [ONLINE] Available at: https://www.pymnts.com/news/retail/2021/amazon-walmart-nearly-tied-in-full-year-share-of-retail-sales/

represents an increasingly large percentage of online retail spending, store owners now find themselves adopting business models increasingly reliant on access to this captured audience of online shoppers. With the development of its "marketplace" ecosystem, many entrepreneurs and online retailers took advantage of the huge market of attention and users provided (and controlled) by Amazon.

These small online businesses often find themselves in a difficult situation. With Amazon sales gradually coming to represent an increasing percentage of their total revenue, they become exposed to a set of existential threats that only exist on the Amazon platform.

In one example, pioneers in profitable new or trending product categories have even sometimes found themselves out-competed by Amazon itself, who some claim develop copycat products they then sell at a lower price and promote as much as they want with all the power of their platform.

In the 2020 Wall Street Journal article titled *"How Amazon Wins: By Steamrolling Rivals and Partners"*,[23] this practice is detailed, including a high-profile case where successful environmentally-friendly footwear brand *AllBirds* discovered Amazon to be offering nearly identical versions of their products. AllBirds CEO Joey Zwillinger states in the article *"You can't help but look at a trillion-dollar company putting their muscle and their pockets and their machinations of their algorithms and reviewers and private-label machine all behind something that you've put your career against"*.

The comment offered by Amazon regarding the controversy was somewhat terse: *"Offering products inspired by the trends to which customers are responding is a common practice across the retail industry"*. At this point, it should be expected; you don't become the largest online retailer in the world without a spirit of competition. In a 2012 interview with Fortune magazine, Amazon founder Jeff Bezos is famous for having himself said, *"Your margin is my opportunity"*.[24]

---

[23] Dana Mattioli. How Amazon Wins: By Steamrolling Rivals and Partners - WSJ [ONLINE] Available at: https://www.wsj.com/articles/amazon-competition-shopify-wayfair-allbirds-antitrust-11608235127

[24] Fortune.com. Amazon's Jeff Bezos: The Ultimate Disrupter | Fortune [ONLINE] Available at: https://fortune.com/2012/11/16/amazons-jeff-bezos-the-ultimate-disrupter/

It's unlikely there will be any challengers to Amazon's grip on online retail, and these practices will likely continue. In spite of European Union Antitrust allegations focused on precisely this intra-platform competition with its own sellers,[25] there are new claims of the company manipulating the visibility of smart-home products which compete with Amazon's own Echo and Fire product lines.[26]

While an outside observer may easily see the risks of building a model reliant on Facebook and Amazon, for other platforms this risk is less readily apparent.

Google

Google probably holds just as much of this platform risk as those just mentioned, though it's seemingly less often acknowledged. At time of writing, tens of thousands of small online businesses have built traffic strategies almost entirely reliant on "organic" sources, or in other words, from ranking highly in Google search results. But this term "organic traffic", adopted by the multi-billion dollar Search Engine Optimization (SEO) industry, is something of a misnomer. Platform risk is just as easily found here.

In one example, a 2019 update to the Google algorithm reoriented its focus to favor established authority sources - often large incumbents from the previous world of print - pushing out smaller players and rendering the previously generous traffic source less so than before. While these updates were said to be part of an effort to help combat unreliable information sources, the rollout of sweeping algorithmic changes often proves less than perfect.

Independent nutrition and supplementation knowledge website *Examine.com*, long recognized as an authority in the space providing

---

[25] Ec.europa.eu. Antitrust: EC opens formal investigation against Amazon [ONLINE] Available at: https://ec.europa.eu/commission/presscorner/detail/pl/ip_19_4291

[26] Dana Mattioli, Patience Haggin and Shane Shifflett. Amazon Restricts How Rival Device Makers Buy Ads on Its Site - WSJ [ONLINE] Available at: https://www.wsj.com/articles/amazon-restricts-advertising-competitor-device-makers-roku-arlo-11600786638?mod=article_inline

detailed summaries of peer-reviewed articles on the topic, reported in February 2020 that recent Google updates had reduced their organic traffic by around ~90%. Kamal Patel, the site's founder and operator for nearly ten years, laments in the article, *"Alas, it seems that, in Google's battle against the immense amount of misinformation and outright lies in the health space, Examine.com has been caught in the crossfire"*.[27]

Within their rights to do so, like Amazon, Google also allegedly influences its search results with the intention of stifling emerging competitors. After an attempted purchase of restaurant reviews company *Yelp* by Google in 2009,[28] CEO Jeremy Stoppelman spoke out at a 2012 Business Insider conference[29] regarding Google's attempts to outcompete them by reducing their search visibility. Regarding the practices, he said *"If you happen to be the gateway for the vast majority of users on the Internet and you restrict information and put your house property ahead of everyone else, you potentially harm consumers … We can all agree that's probably not a good thing."* Whatever Google's intentions, it's evident it can be just as risky as the other platforms.

The Walled Gardens

What makes platform risk so insidious is it often remains hidden until it's too late. This is why understanding its prevalence and how easily it can destroy a business overnight is so important. How can we avoid the same fate as Hayley?

Comparing the periods before and after the arrival of the internet, it's clear there's been a dramatic shift in the way businesses must operate. But this shift is somewhat under acknowledged and is likely a large part of the reason so many find themselves in similar situations.

---

[27] Examine.com. Why has Examine.com disappeared from search results? | Examine.com [ONLINE] Available at: https://examine.com/nutrition/google-update-july-2019/
[28] Techcrunch.com. Google In Discussions To Acquire Yelp For A Half Billion Dollars Or More | TechCrunch [ONLINE] Available at: https://techcrunch.com/2009/12/17/google-acquire-buy-yelp/
[29] Businessinsider.com. Google Wants to Kill Yelp [ONLINE] Available at: https://www.businessinsider.com/google-wants-to-kill-yelp-2012-12?IR=T

Fittingly, the name sometimes used to describe this phenomenon of large, dominant platforms controlling exclusive access to the vast majority of internet audiences has been referred to as the "Walled Gardens".[30,31,32]

It describes how these platforms such as Amazon, Facebook, or Google have built their own closed-off data ecosystems, independent from the rest of the internet. By gathering data privately for their own benefit, Walled Garden platforms oppose the "openness" that characterized the early ideals of the internet (or most information technologies for that matter, as Wu's history retells).

While incentivizing internet users to gather on their platforms isn't a problem in itself, their increasingly closed-off character is what earns them their namesake.

One feature of a Walled Garden is the discouragement of users from venturing off-platform into the wider internet. As one 2015 Forbes article described the problem, using Facebook as an example: *"Facebook's goal is, understandably, to keep users happy and engaged in its own garden. The longer we spend there, the more the company learns about us — and the more ads it can deliver."*[33]

This is the reason platform risk exists in the first place. As they gather more users and deeper insights about their behavior, the Walled Gardens can compound their appeal to new users. At the same time, those who create the content that fuels their growth fall into a corresponding cycle of dependency.

---

[30] Seekingalpha.com. Programmatic Advertising: Walled Gardens May Be The Real Winners | Seeking Alpha [ONLINE] Available at: https://seekingalpha.com/article/4332959-programmatic-advertising-walled-gardens-may-be-real-winners

[31] Warc.com. Walled gardens are the future for brands | WARC [ONLINE] Available at: https://www.warc.com/newsandopinion/news/walled-gardens-are-the-future-for-brands/42981

[32] Tech-bytes.net. Walled gardens are growing taller: Platform lock-in — Tech Bytes - Articles - Tech Bytes [ONLINE] Available at: https://tech-bytes.net/posts/2017/10/9/walled-gardens-are-growing-taller

[33] Sachin Kamdar. 3 Things About Walled Gardens That Drive Digital Publishers 'Up The Wall' [ONLINE] Available at: https://www.forbes.com/sites/sachinkamdar/2015/10/18/3-things-about-walled-gardens-that-drive-digital-publishers-up-the-wall/?sh=224d9d634aae

As these "information empires" inevitably gather power, the height of the walls around their gardens is only likely to increase. While the garden inside the walls grows more verdant, the space outside of them slowly becomes a wasteland. To avoid platform risk, we need a broader understanding of how these Walled Gardens have amassed so much power in the first place. As a small online business owner, it's important to know what you're up against.

Aggregation: How Walled Gardens Grow

When information is cheap, attention becomes expensive.
James Gleick, *The Information*

There's a simple way to explain exactly how these Walled Gardens have become so prominent. In a 2015 article *"Aggregation Theory"*, tech-industry commentator Ben Thompson outlines the strategy large tech companies have used to quickly become powerful centers of audiences and attention.

It's helpful to model a consumer market as made up of three interacting parts:

1. **The suppliers** of a service or product.
2. **The distributors** that connect those suppliers to the market.
3. **The consumers** who demand the product.

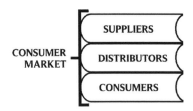

A breakdown of consumer markets.

Thompson explains the ways a business can gain competitive advantage and dominate a consumer market are to either:

(i) **"gain a horizontal monopoly in one of the three parts"** – completely control any one of these segments of (1) supply, (2) distribution or (3) consumer demand.

Or,

(ii) **"integrate two of the parts such that you have a competitive advantage in delivering a vertical solution"** – instead of completely controlling any *one* aspect, gain access to any *two* aspects: either integrate a (1) *supply* with a means of (2) *distribution*; or integrate a means of (2) *distribution* with access to (3) *consumer* demand.

Two primary ways to gain competitive advantage.

This sounds a bit overly abstract. But it's important to visualize in order to understand the shift that has occurred since the arrival of the internet.

Pre-Internet Business

Historically, the most profitable businesses were those that either maintained (i) "horizontal" monopolies over distribution, or who provided (ii) an "integrated vertical solution" combining distribution with access to a means of supplying it.

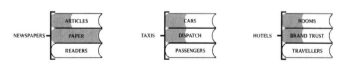

Successful pre-internet business models.

Newspapers, as one example, were dominant in the pre-internet era due to monopolizing distribution for a local news area, while also "integrating" the supply of information and news via journalism. This combined (i) a local distribution monopoly, with (ii) an integrated vertical solution that connected supply. The profits in this case were made by offering advertising to the captured market.

The publishing industry is another example. By controlling the distribution of books and signing the authors writing those books, publishers could capture profits through this (ii) integrated vertical solution, despite no single publisher owning a complete monopoly over either the supply, distribution or demand for books.

Other examples include hotels, which integrated (ii) the supply of vacant rooms with the distribution of those rooms via trusted brand names, and taxi companies which integrated (ii) a supply of cars with a distribution system consisting of "medallion" that signaled trust, with a central dispatch process.

So, the pre-internet era could be characterized by dominant companies controlling either supply or distribution advantages. But with the arrival of the internet, this formula was flipped on its head.

Post-Internet Business

Whereas an advantage had previously been gained by integrating distribution and supply, this has now shifted to favoring an "integrated vertical solution" that combines distribution with access to end consumers.

Amazon, Facebook and Google are prime examples of this shift. Instead of firms competing with one another for exclusive access to supplier relationships, the supply side has now become the commodity.

Content publishers, the new suppliers, are now scrambling to use the distribution methods these companies control in order to access their unprecedented access to consumers. A 2015 article describes this "*Faustian Bargain*", with the benefits of additional advertising revenue and readership being offset by a ceding of power: *"Media companies don't really have a choice. They are forced to work with Facebook whether they want to or not, because the platform plays such a huge role in how millions of people come into contact with the news.'*[84]

The lesson to be learned from the Walled Gardens is that the most successful companies today all seek to treat the end-consumer as the new first-order priority. Whichever platform provides the best user experience will end up attracting the majority of their market. As Thompson explains, "… *the best distributors/aggregators/ market-makers win by providing the best experience, which earns them the most consumers/users, which attracts the most suppliers, which enhances the user experience in a virtuous cycle*".

In contrast to the examples given of pre-internet companies, this new strategy can be seen in the models adopted by contemporary household-name companies:

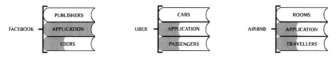

Successful post-internet business models.

- **Uber**
  Infamous for its rapid disruption of the taxi industry, Uber integrated a means of distribution (its app) with direct access to consumer demand (app users).

  By providing a superior user experience (cheaper fares, more trust and nicer cars) it gained consumer demand and in turn supplanted the incumbent taxi industry.

  The result of their successful integration of distribution and demand was the unlocking of an existing, but previously inaccessible supply commodity – the millions of under-used, privately owned cars that fuel the uber app.

---

[34] Finance.yahoo.com. Should News Sites Make a 'Faustian Bargain' With Facebook? [ONLINE] Available at: https://finance.yahoo.com/news/should-news-sites-make-a-faustian-bargain-with-114596098814.html?guccounter=1

- **Airbnb**
  Similarly disruptive to existing hoteliers, Airbnb again vertically integrated distribution (its app) with direct access to consumer demand.

  By providing a superior user experience (cheaper accommodation, more options and an "authentic"[35] travel experience) it gained consumer demand and in turn created a brand new, and highly competitive, accommodation category.

  The result of their successful integration of distribution and demand was, again, the unlocking of an existing but previously hidden supply commodity – the millions of vacant apartments and spare rooms that now drive the listings on their site and app.

- **Facebook**
  As we've touched on briefly, Facebook used this same playbook to disrupt the traditional news publishing industry. They control both a powerful distribution mechanism (the news feed) vertically integrated with direct access to consumer demand (their massive user base).

  As with the other example, it first gained this demand by providing a superior user experience (a central source of social information, as well as an easy portal to the internet for older users). It has then been able to use this attention advantage to broker publisher supply of news to its billions of users.

  The result of their successful integration of distribution and demand created a new supply commodity – the news content previously offered by traditional publishers on their own platforms.

---

[35] Npr.org. Airbnb: Joe Gebbia : How I Built This with Guy Raz : NPR [ONLINE] Available at: https://www.npr.org/2017/10/19/543035808/airbnb-joe-gebbia

So how are small business owners expected to compete with such large companies? With names like Uber, Facebook and Airbnb used as examples, the idea may seem far-fetched.

While any person can still create their own website or application, the current situation would have it seem the viability of their venture is ultimately limited by its relationship and access to one of these Walled Gardens. What hope does a small business really have? Like Hayley, you can now set up an eCommerce store in less than a day - but where are you going to find customers? Having known the risks upfront, could Hayley *really* have done anything differently? If she didn't build her audience on Instagram, where else would she have done so?

When Hayley was starting out, there was seemingly little alternative. The early success of her business depended on working behind the walls of one of these increasingly verdant gardens of attention, users and prospective customers. Without first building an audience on Instagram, she never could have started her business in the first place.

So does knowing what we've just covered actually do anything for us? Like Hayley, surely we don't have any option but to rely on the audiences of these existing companies? With this view, never before has starting a business been so seemingly fraught with danger.

But a solution does exist. I don't present this information just to increase your anxiety. There are thousands of successful small online businesses in operation today, all of whom have found a way to compete with the Walled Gardens.

As they show, there is a way to offset our exposure to platform risk. Like any risk, properly understanding it is the first step towards mitigating it. Now that we understand how the Walled Gardens have amassed so much influence, let's look at where we can fit in as small online business owners using email marketing.

II. ...or, Optimism

The beginning of the industrial revolution - the onset of modernity - was a tumultuous period. Existing ways of life were being disrupted, new ideas were emerging, and like today, there was mixed sentiment to the widespread changes.

In many ways, the atmosphere of the time mirrored the mix of reservation and awe toward technology we have today. As media theorist Marshall McLuhan remarked in 1962, *"We are today as far into the electric age as the Elizabethans had advanced into the typographical and mechanical age. And we are experiencing the same confusions and indecisions which they had felt when living simultaneously in two contrasted forms of society and experience".*[36]

While the tumult was similar, there was then a greater sense of optimism for the promises of the emerging technologies. Art critic Robert Hughes writes of the period in "The Shock of the New" saying, *"… only very exceptional sights, like a rocket launch, can give us anything resembling the emotion with which our ancestors in the 1880s contemplated heavy machinery. For them, the "romance" of technology seemed far more diffused and optimistic, acting publicly on a wider range of objects, than it is today".*[37]

But not all were so optimistic. French intellectual Voltaire didn't share this "romance" of his later contemporaries. He was skeptical of the arrival of some vague Eden by way of what some critics referred to as a "technical society".[38][39] Struck one day by inspiration, it is said that Voltaire wrote his most famous work, "Candide or The Optimist"[40], across three restless days and nights. Later becoming one of the most famous works of the 18th century, "Candide" would satirize these seemingly paradisiacal promises of technology.

---

[36] McLuhan, M. (1969) The Gutenberg Galaxy. Signet Book.

[37] Hughes, R. (1991) The shock of the new: Art and the century of change. London, England: Thames & Hudson.

[38] Barrett, W. (1979) Illusion of Technique. Glasgow, Scotland: HarperCollins Distribution Services.

[39] Ellul, J. (1973) The Technological Society. New York, NY: Random House.

[40] Voltaire (1968) Candide. Edited by J. H. Brumfitt. London, England: Oxford University Press.

A central lesson comes towards the books' end, when the characters come across a peaceful farmer sitting beneath a tree outside his small estate. Asking the old man if he heard any details about a recent calamity in the nearby capitol, the farmer answers that he does not know. He adds he doesn't care, *"I never bother with what is going on in Constantinople"*.

The old man invites Candide and his companions into his home, where they're amazed by the bounty he has to offer. Thinking surely this must be a very wealthy man, Candide inquires how much land the old man owns, to which he responds *"I have only twenty acres ... I and my children cultivate them; and our labor preserves us from three great evils: weariness, vice and want"*.

Candide, impressed by what he had seen, later reflects to his traveling companions *"This honest Turk ... seems to be in a far better place than kings ..."*, and here is the novel's famous line: *"... we (too) must cultivate our garden"*.

More than two hundred years later, as our time mirrors that of Voltaire's, the advice from "Candide" is more relevant than ever. "Candide" confers the importance of our responsibility to create our own immediate Eden, rather than relying on the promise of one materializing from social or technological progress.

The vast information empires seem to build increasingly high walls guarding their privileged gardens of information. Yet while access to their fecund private audiences is protected, there is still an opportunity to cultivate new gardens of our own.

The Walled Gardens propose a grim future for the internet; there's no escaping the reality of the current online business environment. But with the right approach, it would have been possible for Hayley to maintain everything she had worked for: her growing profits, delighted customers, and her fulfilling lifestyle of flexibility, wealth and independence.

It's all about allowing the audiences of these monolithic internet entities to find a new home in a Walled Garden that *you* manage and control. Somewhere on their perimeter, there is still space where you can mark out your own patch - your own "20 acres" - to build profitable, sustainable businesses. But this "perimeter", the exact location of construction, is an important detail. The way we go about finding success with marketing on the internet is by building in the correct location.

How to Cultivate a Walled Garden

Before finally arriving at the solution, let's break down some fundamentals to understand this better. When we refer to "the internet" we must remember this is actually something of a catch-all term referring to a collection of distinct processes.

These processes, the core mechanics for retrieving information over a computer network, are known collectively as the "Internet Protocol Suite" (TCP/IP). TCP/IP is so named as its two dominant, defining protocols are Transmission Control Protocol (TCP) and Internet Protocol (IP).

TCP/IP then has subcategories of all protocols essential to running the internet grouped across four "layers":

1. **The Link Layer** protocols help establish initial connections.

2. **The Internet Layer** protocols help build a network between these connections'

3. **The Transport Layer** protocols help to provide a more reliable connection to move data more effectively.

4. **The Application Layer** offers more specialized protocols that help translate your interactions with the web into data back down into the other layers.

The above is a (very) simplified description of the architecture of the internet. The reason I describe this is due to the necessity of understanding *where* exactly inside this architecture the prevailing Walled Gardens have been built. The important thing to understand is that the various protocols are broken down into four different groupings based on the distinct purposes they serve.

In a 2016 blog post, Joel Monegro, a partner at venture capital fund Unity Square Ventures, describes exactly this. In the article, he describes his view of the value, from an investor's perspective, of these different protocol layers; the majority of protocols being "thin" in value and the application layer in particular being "fat".

In the post, he describes how in the post-internet era the majority of value created by large companies such as Amazon, Facebook or Google has all occurred within the fourth "fat" protocol – *the Application Layer.*

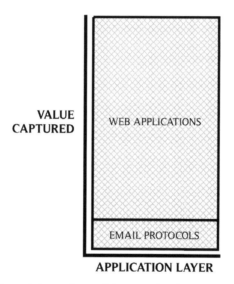

Value on the internet has mostly been created on the applications layer.

Monegro describes "*As the market developed, [our fund] learned that investing in applications produced high returns whereas investing directly in protocol technologies generally produced low returns.*"[41]

Airbnb, Facebook, Amazon, Instagram, WhatsApp, TikTok and Twitter have one thing in common – they're all web applications. They all depend

---

[41] Usv.com. Fat Protocols | Union Square Ventures [ONLINE] Available at: https://www.usv.com/writing/2016/08/fat-protocols/

on the same tiny slice of the Application Layer. In this case, the value created by these Walled Gardens each sit atop just a few Application Layer protocols - such as HTML and HTTPS. These large companies have built massively valuable businesses *on top* of just a few handful of protocols used to access and display web pages.

But the Application Layer isn't limited to just the protocols used by the current Walled Gardens, HTML and HTTPS.

There are dozens of others, with many so far relatively untouched. It's exactly in these other protocols where we find those used for the delivery of email - SMTP, POP3 and IMAP. These are all protocols on the Application Layer that have been relatively untouched by the significant value creation seen over the past two decades.

The inexorable force of Wu's Kronos Effect has so far failed to swallow up email. This powerful technology, used every day by billions of people, has incredibly stayed mostly immune from the reliable warring of information empires.

This reveals a new frontier free for the taking. Instead of competing on the HTML and HTTPS layers we can instead turn to new lands. We can do as the old farmer instructs and *"cultivate our own garden*. With little competition, email presents small online business owners the unique opportunity to build a Walled Garden of their own.

Foundation: Rethinking the Website

With an understanding of the Walled Gardens, platform risk and the protocol layers, this should shift the way we think about building a business online. This is especially true with regards to the function of our website.

We spend a lot of time finding ways to get more traffic. The expectation, more often than not, is that if the website is optimized for whatever action you want that traffic to take, then that is the action they will take.

It's assumed that if you put your store's products front and center, a certain percentage of the traffic you send to your site will purchase them. Similarly, we assume that if you include a button to "book a demo" for your software, some of the traffic you send to your site will end up clicking the button to set up a time to chat.

But this basic assumption couldn't be farther from the truth. A large percentage of this traffic will never take the desired action. Most visitors will not do the things you wish they would. This is evidenced simply through the amount of traffic that leaves a site, often measured as the bounce rate. As of 2021 the industry-wide bounce-rate for a website is 61%.[42] This means less than 40% of the traffic that comes to your site is actually navigating to a second page after first arriving.

What this shows is the vast majority of your traffic *isn't ready* to buy a product upon the first visit to your site. They haven't yet bought into the narrative of your brand to be excited enough to actually want to buy anything from you. They don't know enough about your software to "book a demo". They don't care enough about your services to "send an inquiry".

So, what happens when they don't take the desired action? They leave your site, and often never return. This creates massive inefficiency and lost potential. So we end up spending more and more time "getting traffic", sending it into a black box and praying for "conversions", with all those visitors completely uncaptured.

The thinking is fundamentally flawed. By attempting to grow your business this way, like Hayley, you're stepping right into the role of a vassal for a Walled Garden. You'll spend all your time on different traffic strategies, and then when you finally get it, it'll be a flash in the pan. The solution, and the aim of this book, is to instruct you on how to cultivate your own garden – how to leverage the lessons of the aggregators to compete in a way that is more effective.

---

[42] Growrevenue.io. What's a good bounce rate? (Here's the average bounce rate for websites) - GrowRevenue.io [ONLINE] Available at: https://growrevenue.io/bounce-rate-benchmarks/

The first step towards this is rethinking the function of your website. Consider from this point on that the primary function of your site is to capture email addresses. This seems aggressive, but it's not. You must have a serious plan for converting the visitors on your site into email subscribers. Every visitor is a potential subscriber, every subscriber is then a potential customer.

STAGE	FOUNDATION	DISPERSAL	RECRUITMENT	ESTABLISHMENT
GOAL	TSC	Engagement	Conversion	Lifetime Value
METHOD	Improve Optin Placements	Provide Value / Progress Awareness	Personalization	Increase New Orders / Increase Repeat Orders / Increase Average Order Value
AUTOMATIONS	N/A	Awareness Automation	Semantic Automation	LTV Automation

The way this is sometimes delineated is the distinction between a Marketing-Qualified Lead and a Sales-Qualified Lead. A Marketing-Qualified Lead, in sales terminology, is someone within your target market who could potentially become a customer at some point. They must be nurtured and educated to the point where they can become ready to be sold to, or in other words graduate to becoming a Sales-Qualified Lead.

The distinction is important. When traffic is sent to your site from a Walled Garden, these are almost always Marketing-Qualified Leads. They know little of your business or what you offer and are generally unlikely to take the conversion action you want them to take (buying products, booking demos, etc). So the focus needs to be on capturing these Marketing-Qualified leads for further education.

So the main function of your site is to be a machine for gathering such leads. You must make sure the traffic that comes to your site is captured. Only in doing so can we have a chance of nurturing our subscribers to the point where they'll take action on our product or services. But how do we do this?

Traffic to Subscriber Conversion

When taking this new perspective, one metric is more important than all others when it comes to your website – Traffic to Subscriber conversion (TSC).

This is simply a measure of the percentage of traffic that converts to new email list subscribers: if 1000 visitors come to your site and you add 100 subscribers, your TSC is 10%.

From an email marketing perspective, it's the only metric that really matters on your website. All other site metrics are simply factors that lead to this: bounce rate, time on page, scroll percentage or any other metric you can think of each only require improvement in context of how they impact your TSC.

By focusing on improving TSC, you're making sure you're getting the most value possible out of the traffic you send to your site. Doing so can even become a potential source of competitive advantage. The majority of sites are severely under-optimized in this area, with the average TSC conversion a paltry 1.95%.[43] This means that for every 1000 visitors, the average site only converts 19 of them to subscribers. What's more, the top 10% of marketers will only ever achieve a TSC of around 4.77%. So if you can beat those quite low figures, you'll be in the top percentage of sites.

What advantage does it yield, exactly? You'll be able to get more subscribers, with less traffic. This frees up time for more impactful marketing activities that aren't just trying to extract site visitors from Walled Gardens.

It's always easier to optimize the conversion of existing traffic than it is to actually get more traffic. Think about it: if you're getting 10000 uniques per month to a specific page right now with a TSC of 5%, that generates 50 new subscribers. In order to get to 100 subscribers per

---

[43] Sumo Group, Inc.. Email Signup Benchmarks: How Many Visitors Should Be Converting [ONLINE] Available at: https://sumo.com/stories/email-signup-benchmarks

month, you can either double your traffic (very hard) or double your optin conversion rate (relatively easy).

Of course, a balance must be struck. You don't want to relentlessly optimize toward TSC and ignore everything else.

How to Get More Subscribers (without being annoying)

Have you ever visited a site only to have your attention bombarded with dozens of popups? If you've been on the internet in the past decade, I'm sure you know what I'm talking about. You know the ones: "Sign up to our newsletter", "Enter your email to access our 10 tips to get more traffic", "Download this free PDF with more info". They all share one thing in common: they're annoying.

These "popups" are notorious for destroying your brand experience, and your site visitors generally view them as aggressive, intrusive and distracting. Because they are.

Why do we put them there then? It's like a customer walking into a store and prompting them to fill out a form before even saying "hello". Terrible brand experience. The worst are those that fill your screen suddenly, forcing you to close out of them. Other contenders are those ones that slide in from the side of the screen, obstructing the text you were viewing or impeding what you originally came to the site to do.

This may sound surprising reading this in a book about email marketing automation: but most optin forms suck. Sure, these methods can improve your TSC to an extent, but improving that metric with tactics like these come with a hidden cost. For every subscriber you convert, a large percentage of potential customers get annoyed with your site and leave.

In a 2016 blog post titled *"I'm killing most of my email capture. Here's why"*, marketing agency owner Nat Eliason discovered some of these hidden costs: *"I recently purged a portion of my email list, realizing that there were old signups who were inactive. Before I deleted them, I went through their information and found something interesting: almost 100% of the inactive subscribers were the ones who signed up through a content upgrade or lead magnet."* [44]

The point the author makes in the article isn't that aggressive optin forms are necessarily bad (he even concedes that certain business models *should* show some aggression in this area), but that they can create an illusion of success by optimizing for a metric that ultimately doesn't yield any longer term gain, as in his example. By being overly aggressive, you risk building a large list of inactive users, at the cost of your brand experience and first impressions for site visitors and potential customers.

There's a fine line between annoying your subscribers and being helpful, and it's clear a balance must be struck. Many would agree that highly aggressive optin forms are annoying, and they hurt the first impressions of your brand. So what strategy should we use to still optimize our website for TSC, without annoying users and creating a poor experience?

I have three optin form placements I think anyone can implement that do just that. They strike a good balance between actively optimizing for TSC and being highly visible, while at the same time avoiding being obnoxious or obtrusive for site visitors. The idea is that with the following form placements, you won't be annoying your subscribers, you'll actually be offering additional value. I recommend you add opportunities to join your email list in the following places:

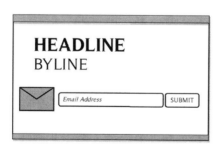

Site Homepage Optin

---

[44] Nateliason.com. I'm killing most of my email capture. Here's why. - Nat Eliason [ONLINE] Available at: https://www.nateliason.com/blog/email-capture

I. Site Homepage: When a visitor arrives at your site, don't use slide-in forms or popup-screens that take up the whole page. Instead, make sure there is simply an opportunity to stay up to date with an option form immediately available.

A site homepage is typically structured with a headline which captures initial attention and states the main benefit of the brand. This is followed by a byline: a further explanation of that benefit which ties it back to the subscriber.

The place for a Site Homepage form is below the byline. After stating how the benefit of the site is related to the visitor, all you need to do is mention that there is an opportunity to stay up to date, and place the form there. A retail hedge fund uses this technique to pique the interest of site visitors.[45]

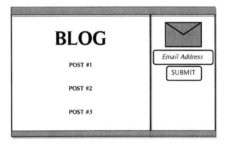

Blog Archive Page Optin

II. Blog Archive Page: The blog archive page, in a similar way to the homepage optin, simply presents another opportunity to join the email list without being obstructive or annoying.

Think about the role of content marketing. It's generally used as a way to build trust, establish authority and help prospective customers solve common problems. By placing an optin form in this part of your site,

---

[45] Mutinyfund.com. The Mutiny Tail Risk Fund - A Long Volatility Investment Approach [ONLINE] Available at: https://mutinyfund.com/

you provide another opportunity to extend value to your visitor without being aggressive and annoying.

What this and site homepage positioning have in common, is that while they avoid overt attention-seeking tactics, they're still visible and center stage. After all, collecting email addresses should be one of the main functions of the site, so your user experience should reflect its importance.

This fashion eCommerce store shows a good example of a Blog Archive Page optin form.[46]

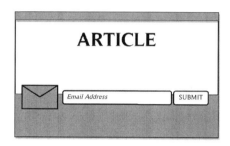

Specific Blog Posts Optin

III. Specific Blog Posts: Finally, each *individual* blog post should give your site visitors a chance to sign up. What's the difference between this form and the "Blog Archive Page" form above? The main difference is that these forms should be highly specific and tailored toward the topic covered in each individual post. Let's look at these in a bit more detail.

Hyper-Specific Optins

One of the most effective ways to improve TSC is by creating highly relevant optins for each unique piece of content that receives traffic. Got a blog post that gets 1000 uniques per month? The best way to

---

[46] Watson & Wolfe. Journal - Listen, Watch & Read Articles to Entertain & Inspire | Watson & Wolfe – Watson & Wolfe [ONLINE] Available at: https://www.watsonwolfe.com/the-journal-blog/

improve TSC would be to create an incentive to subscribe that builds on the value of that article in a meaningful way.

The point is that you dedicate just as long as you took to write that article to building this incentive. Sounds like a lot of work? It's worth it. It may take time, but it's an incredibly high leverage activity - the ROI you'll get from this should rank at the top of your marketing activities list.

This is because these types of Hyper-Specific Optins are the most effective way to improve TSC. I mentioned previously the average TSC was around 1.95%, and the top 10% of marketers only achieve a TSC of around ~5%. But the image below shows an example of some Hyper-Specific Optins that achieve far and above the disappointing average of 1.95%.

The lowest converting optin in the below image is 11.65%, already achieving higher than the supposed "Top 10% of marketers". Better still, the top performing example on the bottom row hits a TSC conversion of more than 20%.

The reason these types of optins are so effective is because they actually create an experience of extra value for the site visitor. They are neither annoying nor aggressive. They build on the value offered in your content marketing efforts and extend an invitation to continue the relationship with your prospect. Importantly, this invite takes place on your email list - not on a Walled Garden you don't control.

So how do you make sure you're building an optin that's actually valuable? In short, focus on helping the subscriber implement something taught or demonstrated in the article in question. A "Free PDF" usually won't cut it. The key to a high performing optin form is to go above and beyond in the value you provide in the article.

Here are some examples of high-performing optins:

- **Tools:** The most effective method I've personally found to improve TSC is by providing a highly specific tool that helps the subscriber implement something taught in a post. From the examples above, the optin achieving upwards of 20% conversion is itself a tool of this kind.

    The article in question explains how to calculate expected value from different marketing activities. The optin is then a spreadsheet that has the entire model from the article built-out inside it.[47] By spending time building a tool that implements the lessons from the article, you do the legwork that they would have had to have done anyway. It creates additional value the visitor is more than happy to exchange an email address for.

- **Quizzes:** Another high-converting opt in incentive that can be tailored to specific articles are quizzes. Quizzes can help subscribers take the education in your articles to the next level and offer them the chance for a personalized and entertaining experience. Providing these sorts of highly-personalized interactions with your site are highly effective, and said to be a large part of the success of internet media giant Buzzfeed.[48]

    You can borrow from that success by providing a way for your visitors to interact with your article via a quiz. For example, marketing-focused quiz software company *Interact* claims almost unbelievable success via their software, stating their quizzes have "*generated over 8 million email subscribers with an average conversion rate of 50%*".[49] What if you could convert 50% of your site's visitors to email addresses?

---

[47] Taylorpearson.me. Improve Your Decision-Making Using an Expected Value Calculator [ONLINE] Available at: https://taylorpearson.me/expected-value-calculator/
[48] Vox.com. BuzzFeed's founder used to write Marxist theory and it explains BuzzFeed perfectly - Vox [ONLINE] Available at: https://www.vox.com/2014/5/20/5730762/buzzfeeds-founder-used-to-write-marxist-theory-and-it-explains
[49] Tryinteract.com. How to Design an Email Opt-in Form That Converts at 50% | Interact Blog [ONLINE] Available at: https://www.tryinteract.com/blog/how-to-design-an-email-opt-in-form-that-converts-at-50/

- **Discounts:** Last but not least, the humble discount is a mainstay for eCommerce stores for a good reason: they work very well. In a survey by CouponScience.org, they found 92% of consumers surveyed reported using a coupon or took advantage of a discount in 2017.[50]

The effectiveness of these discounts is related to their placement. These types of incentives are most effective and have the highest conversions when used in a similar manner to the above: only offer the discount when it's relevant. Use behavioral triggers such as page scroll percentage or on specific pages, to offer discounts that are personalized to the product or category your visitor is viewing.

The Law of Shitty Clickthroughs

With that in mind, it's worth recognizing the phenomenon known as the "Law of Shitty Clickthroughs". Originally coined by Venture Capitalist and startup founder Andrew Chen, the Law simply states that *"Over time, all marketing strategies result in shitty clickthrough rates"*.[51]

An example of this is the traditional "banner ad" seen everywhere in the early days of the internet, the banner ad was highly effective when it first appeared in 1994, *"debuting with a clickthrough rate of 78%"*. The expected conversion rate from a banner ad today is now something in the range of 0.05%, as tested on Facebook by Chen in 2011.

All marketing strategies will eventually be exhausted. As marketers and business owners we must constantly reiterate and redesign our tactics in order to keep up with the times and maintain effectiveness. However, the "Law of Shitty Clickthroughs" applies to granular strategies, not to timeless marketing principles.

---

[50] Couponscience.org. 2019 Coupon and Promo Code Use Study | OHC [ONLINE] Available at: https://couponscience.org/iherb/2017-coupon-promo-code-study/
[51] Andrewchen.com. The Law of Shitty Clickthroughs at andrewchen [ONLINE] Available at: https://andrewchen.com/the-law-of-shitty-clickthroughs/

What I hope to demonstrate over the next few chapters is a system for thinking about marketing strategy that has true staying power. Concepts such as respecting your audience, seeking to constantly provide value, and developing your customers aren't just tactics that will change and fall like leaves. Like the principles of growth we'll copy from nature, these are timeless ideas that have long been central to all successful businesses. The *Natural Orders* system I'll walk through in the following chapters will serve you for years to come.

The "Kronos Effect" posed by the information empires first outlined by Wu in 2011 aren't going anywhere. We are still at the beginning of the Walled Gardens, and this makes things such as email marketing, automation and "cultivating our own garden" more effective and important than ever. We need to build our own ecosystem in order to build a business that can stand on its own.

In the next section, I'm going to walk through exactly how to set up the foundations for such an ecosystem. The Dispersal stage builds upon the emails we've started collecting here to truly create the foundations needed to create a long-lasting business. It's a relatively simple strategy based on timeless marketing techniques, and it ensures you'll get started with email and automation in a way that builds that essential foundation, while also getting some early wins.

Summary

- Throughout history, every new information technology has gone through the same pattern of open and idealistic beginnings, then transitioning to being **closed and controlled by commercial interests**.

- The emergence of "**Walled Gardens**" describes the process of this happening with the internet: key players such as Facebook, Amazon and Google have become dominant institutions that increasingly gain power and control over this new technology.

- Business owners who leverage the internet face new opportunities, but also new challenges. **Platform risk** describes the relatively new phenomena of business owners building the foundations of their businesses atop these platforms, and then being forcibly shut down due to increasing regulation and arbitrary policy changes.

- The answer to the platform risk problem is to "**cultivate our own garden**". We can use email as our answer to the difficult business environment created by the Walled Gardens. By structuring our site with an intention to collect email addresses, we take back control and cultivate a garden of our own where we have a direct relationship with our market.

A Flying Fox (genus: *polycephalus*). Credit: Yuri Gurevich

I.
DISPERSAL

I. Dispersal

Watch the sunset on Australia's East coast and you're likely to see them: first as silhouettes against the twilight, they can be difficult to make out. It's common to mistake them as large birds, with broad wingbeats laboring heavily towards their shared destination.

But up close, it's easier to tell. These "flying foxes", as they're commonly known, aren't birds (or foxes) at all — but giant bats. While they do kind of resemble their namesake with a vaguely canine face, the giveaway is the wingspan, which can stretch up to a meter across.

Each evening, these huge bats gather in the thousands into densely packed "camps", punctuated along the length of Australia's Eastern coastal hinterland, a distance of some fifteen thousand kilometers.

In a major study in 2000 conducted over six years, scientists tracked the movements of the flying foxes across this area. The object of the study was one Northern species in particular. These bats were regularly depleting all their Northern resources, and were being forced to move Southwards in search of food.

Yet despite continual movement into the South, the Northern bats were never successful in securing a more permanent foothold in these resource-rich southern areas. Rather than being able to set up a camp of their own in the South, they constantly had to continue making the journey with each new generation.[52] There was something about the South that just wasn't amenable to the Northern species.

In ecology terms, the Northern population of bats were moving from a *source*, into a *sink*:

- The s*ource* of the Northern species had all the requirements to support ongoing births of that population. There were camps for them in their home region.

---

[52] Michael J. Vardon and Christopher R. Tidemann (2000) "The black flying-fox (Pteropus alecto) in north Australia: juvenile mortality and longevity," Australian Journal of Zoology, 48, pp. 91–97.

- But their newly chosen homes – the *sinks* – were not truly viable on their own. They were never able to truly set up a permanent residence there. Rather than becoming a new *source*, these *sink* populations would always rely on a continual stream of new bats from the original *source*.

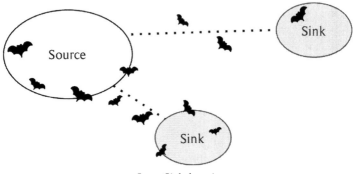

Source-Sink dynamics.

These *source-sink dynamics* are a well observed phenomenon in the world of Ecology. Just as I found certain terms from ecology perfectly described processes in email and automation, *source-sink dynamics* have a clear implication outside of the movement of flying foxes. They also apply to how we build our own ecosystem, our own "Walled Garden".

How can we make sure we build a *source* that thrives on its own? How do we avoid building a *sink* that never becomes self-sustaining?

Dispersal

The underlying movement between these *sources* and *sinks* is known as *Dispersal*. Put simply, dispersal describes the process of organisms seeking out new places to live. If the new environment isn't a great place to live (a *sink*), that generation never gains a foothold there. If the new environment is suitable (and becomes a *source*), the new generation will set up shop and send their succeeding generation into further virgin territory again.

I. Dispersal

It's nature's way of pushing the limits of spatial boundaries, without individual organisms having to move that far within their single lifespans. For example, when rabbits were introduced to the Australian mainland in 1859, it only took fifty years for them to spread across the full extent of the 7.7 million square kilometer continent. This was despite large areas being desert, as well as all considerable human efforts taken to mitigate the spread. This included the release of rabbit-specific viruses and building continent-spanning "rabbit-proof fences" — both tactics proving to be ultimately unsuccessful.

So, Dispersal can be quite powerful. And it also applies to our email list. Unlike rabbits, the reason the Northern bats are "Northern" is because there is something about the South that stops them from spreading there permanently. In an email list, the reason people optin but then leave a few months later works on the same premise. There's something that makes it not a great place to be long term.

On the other hand, a healthy email list is one where someone becomes a subscriber and sticks around for a long time. So we must make sure we're building a *source* rather than a *sink*. With this view, the Walled Gardens of Facebook, Google or Amazon are all *sources* in the way they play host to the vast majority of users on the internet.

The Dispersal stage is all about making sure our email list ecosystem has similar foundations in place to make it more likely that it becomes a *source*. But how exactly will we do this? Why are the Walled Gardens so successful at this? How can we replicate it?

In the previous chapter, we encouraged our site visitors to subscribe by improving TSC. By collecting email addresses, we've opened the gate to allow Dispersal. But we now need to make sure those subscribers stick around. The way we'll do that, and the goal of the Dispersal stage, is *Engagement*. By creating actual incentives to open and read your emails, subscribers are less likely to leave, or unsubscribe.

The way we'll go about maximizing engagement to every new subscriber on your list will be to focus on three pillars of messaging:

1. Educating.
2. Inspiring.
3. Entertaining.

To do this, we'll employ a tried-and-tested framework for understanding what content to send your audience to improve the likelihood they'll interact with our emails. Only with the foundations set can we take the first steps towards the more advanced strategies in the chapters that follow.

STAGE	FOUNDATION	DISPERSAL	RECRUITMENT	ESTABLISHMENT
GOAL	TSC	Engagement	Conversion	Lifetime Value
METHOD	Improve Optin Placements	Provide Value Progress Awareness	Personalization	Increase New Orders Increase Repeat Orders Increase Average Order Value
AUTOMATIONS	N/A	Awareness Automation	Semantic Automation	LTV Automation

Engagement: Solving the Top-Down Cascade

Don't you hate it when you sign up for a new app or newsletter and get bombarded with emails you aren't interested in? At least for me, getting spammed with dozens of promotions straight off the bat is a great way to get me to hit the unsubscribe button.

Helping countless businesses design and build email automation strategies over the years, I've found there's a common thread behind those who struggle to see ROI from email: many are guilty of asking too much and giving too little. Too many offers, too many promotions, too many asks; and in every case, simply not enough value for their subscribers.

With the way many businesses send emails, combined with the sheer volume with which they're sent, it becomes easy to see why many non-marketers harbor something of a quiet disdain for marketing emails.

The way I sometimes describe communicating with an email is this: If you have an email list of 50,000 subscribers, that's the equivalent of a small stadium of people. What do you think will happen if you stand up in front of this crowd and ask them to buy your product with no introduction, no attempt to build any rapport? What if you do this every time? I reckon they'll hate you.

Don't do this. When someone who has trusted us to provide value to them quits the relationship by unsubscribing, it can only be interpreted as a failure to meet expectations. They thought they were going to receive one form of value from you; instead, they received emails that weren't relevant, or even worse, simply annoying.

Consider the perspective of a new subscriber. Having just signed up to your email list (perhaps in exchange for an incentive such as a discount code or free download), they're now ready to be introduced to your brand and, ideally, the problems you can help them solve. Instead, what often occurs is they're immediately hit with a "buy now" email for a product they're not convinced they want or even need.

The result of sending irrelevant or unhelpful information at this critical early stage is invariably the same: poor engagement. This is the reason brands often start out with decent engagement metrics with 25% or higher open rates, but over time see them gradually diminish. After not too long, they find themselves struggling to maintain a 10% open rate, making it extremely difficult to get as much value from your list.

The Engagement-Retention Feedback Loop

By sending emails that fail to provide value, you increase the likelihood of them hitting the unsubscribe button at the bottom of your message. If this happens in great enough numbers over time, departures soon begin to outpace replacements – "mortalities" become greater than "births".

If you can't increase the amount of new subscribers being added to your database to keep up with the corresponding increase in unsubscribes, your list begins to shrink. Rather than going from rocks to grass to shrubs, as the stages of succession instruct, your email list sinks backward into the more basic state of rock and lichen.

Just like a natural ecosystem, your email list begins to collapse "top-down", in a chain of events. The mechanism driving this collapse is Ciller's *feedback loops* we covered earlier.[53] Specifically, it's the feedback loop that occurs between engagement and retention that determines the overall health of your email marketing ecosystem.

The feedback loop begins with poor engagement:

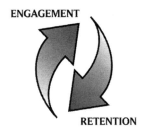

- **Low engagement**: When we send emails that aren't relevant, we create low engagement. This means less people opening or interacting with each email we send.

- **Poor retention**: But engagement indicates whether what we're sending is valuable to our subscribers. So with low engagement, high unsubscribes inevitably follow. With increased unsubscribes, we soon require even more new subscribers to replace them.

---

[53] Serc.carleton.edu. Introduction to Complex Systems [ONLINE] Available at: https://serc.carleton.edu/NAGTWorkshops/complexsystems/introduction.html#feedback

But by simply ensuring you keep your engagement high and focus on always delivering value, you'll keep unsubscribes on the low side and avoid the ecosystem death spiral. It soon becomes obvious why the industry-wide email open rate average is a paltry 14%.

But by compounding beneficial outcomes, we can build a system with better overall "health". This is why it's so important to begin your email marketing automation strategy with the Dispersal stage. But how exactly do we make sure we're setting our subscribers up for strong engagement?

The Simple Way to Improve Engagement

Luckily, the remedy to poor engagement and the ecosystem death spiral that comes with it is relatively straightforward. Think: do you consistently see open rates below 20%? If yes, then from this point on you need to make a few simple changes:

- No more company updates or "what I've been up to" emails.
- No more offers, discounts, deals, promotions (for now).

The key to the mindset shift is this: *Nobody cares!* Your audience doesn't care about your business, or what you've "been up to". subscribers don't care about "company updates" that do nothing to enhance their lives. They definitely don't care about your product that, at this point, doesn't represent anything of value to them.

It's nothing personal - people are just busy. They aren't just individually time-starved, but there's also more competition than ever for your subscriber's attention, a recent study finding *"the average office worker receives 121 emails per day."*[54] If you want to stand out, you must actually have something valuable to draw your subscribers. You must always be creating value in every email you send, and only then will you stand a chance of standing out in the Inbox and gaining the attention, or *engagement*, of your subscribers.

---

[54] Expandedramblings.com. 90 Interesting Facts About Email | How Many Emails are Sent Per Day? [ONLINE] Available at: https://expandedramblings.com/index.php/email-statistics/

I've found the best way to build engagement is by focusing on one of these three things: *educate, inspire, entertain.* By doing at least one of these three things every time you send an email, you focus on creating value for the subscriber.

- **Educate by providing valuable information not found anywhere else.**
  For example: A retail hedge fund sends a weekly email. Inside, they feature conversations with top managers from other funds as a weekly podcast, and break down where they are in the market cycle. Along with this information, they include their fund performance with a CTA to join.

- **Inspire with solutions to problems subscribers are struggling with.**
  For example: An author writes books helping tech professionals overcome procrastination and distraction. After subscribing via a quiz on his site, the subscriber receives emails that address their specific weaknesses revealed by the quiz over a four-week period.

- **Entertain and make your emails something to look forward to.**
  For example: A residential real estate agent spends several hours once a fortnight writing a light-hearted, humorous email commenting on the state of the market. Subscribers look forward to them as they are sent only occasionally and are written in an informal, personal way. The agency's latest listings are included at the bottom of each email.

Try something like this next time you send an email to your audience. Before sending, ask yourself, "Does this email educate, inspire or entertain my subscribers?". If the answer is no, or you have to think about it for too long, then *put it away and send something that does*. I guarantee you'll soon be seeing open rates you probably didn't think were possible.

While the industry-standard benchmarks claim an average open rate of 14%, I would be concerned if a client of mine was regularly getting such numbers. Sometimes it's worth ignoring averages, because in this case a 14% open rate sets the bar too low. By focusing on value for new subscribers above all else, you can easily double that average figure, at minimum. Sounds ridiculous? Look at these screenshots to see what focusing on value above all else (with some smart segmentation) can do for your open rates:

Highly Engaged Open Rates.

For reasons I'll address, open rates aren't actually the most reliable (or important) engagement metric to focus on. But as a general rule, I personally consider a healthy and engaged audience to have anything above a 30% average open rate. If you stop reading now and implement this one piece of advice, it alone should do a lot to transform how much value your subscribers get from your emails.

Timing is Everything: How Engagement Leads to Conversion

So the first part of improving engagement is a mindset shift: always provide value with every email you send. But while it's nice to provide value to people, there's one common objection to this: at what point will subscribers actually buy? After all, you're not in the business of educating, inspiring or entertaining an email database. You want to sell products to people who want to buy them.

The objection is valid: there needs to be a point where conversion happens and subscribers buy your products. Focusing on value for new subscribers ensures your subscribers will stay engaged and interested in what you send. But after achieving that engagement, there eventually comes a point where we actually need to start sending offers to turn those subscribers into buyers.

This doesn't change the fact that, from the subscriber's perspective, they should only ever receive emails that appear to them as valuable and helpful. We want to make sure they will be interested in what it is you're selling, and never perceive your pitch as annoying.

There's nothing wrong with sending an offer or promotion email. But the timing in which it is sent can absolutely transform its meaning. When an offer or promotion is seen as annoying, it's only because your subscriber wasn't ready to receive it in the first place. On the other hand, sending an offer with correct timing, for a product that solves a burning problem, will always be viewed as valuable:

- **An email's *relevance* is the difference between spam and value.**
  A fifteen percent discount on an irrelevant product is spam. A well-designed solution to a problem your subscriber doesn't know exists has zero value.

- **In contrast, a discount on a product that solves a burning problem will drive immediate action**. A solution provided to a problem a subscriber is struggling with can be life-changing.

Remember this. The timing with which we send offers is very important. You can send a fantastic offer to the right prospect at the wrong time, and you won't make the sale. On the other hand, you can send a mediocre offer to a mediocre prospect with perfect timing and be much more likely to generate a sale. In general, *poor timing is the best way to guarantee poor sales.*

But how can we determine when an offer email is going to be valuable? How do we make sure we get this timing correct? The way we determine this is based on a subscriber's level of engagement with previous emails we've already sent. By only sending offers and promotions to those who have engaged frequently with your previous emails you increase the likelihood the offer will be warmly received. Instead of looking like spam, your offer emails will be perceived as valuable information.

This is broadly the solution, but it's not the full picture. The full answer to how we'll actually do this lies in an advertising framework dating back to the 1960's.

The Five Awareness States

Active during the golden age of advertising, by the end of his career Eugene M. Schwartz had a resume boasting tens of millions in revenue generated from his work, a long list of classic headlines to his name, and several books published on his topic of expertise: copywriting and advertising.

Among those books is the classic *Breakthrough Advertising*.[55] First published in 1966, it's still referred to frequently by copywriters around the world. Now out of print from major publishers, there was a time when the privilege of owning a second-hand copy of this book would set you back between five to nine hundred dollars (and it'd likely arrive full of notes and highlights courtesy of its previous owner).

---

[55] Schwartz, E. M. (2017) Breakthrough advertising: How to write ads that shatter traditions and sales records. Book on Demand.

One of the most powerful concepts Schwartz provides in the book is the Five States of Prospect Awareness, or the *Five Awareness States*. Put simply, the *Five Awareness States* describes the depth of understanding a subscriber has about your product. Some will understand precisely the way your product benefits them and are ready to buy, while for another, its value isn't clear to them yet.

There's a spectrum of the education prospects require before you can successfully make the sale. The *Five Awareness States* provides all the different points where a given subscriber might sit on that spectrum:

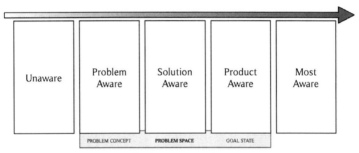

The Five Awareness States

As another legendary copywriter Robert Collier has said, effective copy must *"enter the conversation already going on in your prospect's mind"*.[56] By using the *Five Awareness Sta*tes as reference, you can adjust your messaging so that it meets your subscribers where they're at. In doing so, you make your emails more timely, relevant and valuable, improving engagement and pathing the way to conversion.

With this in mind, the *Five Awareness States* are:

1. Unaware: **Prospect is unaware they have a problem**

Since this person is unaware a problem exists, there's no motivation to solve it. So at this point, your actual product is irrelevant. Describing

---

[56] Collier, R. (2016) The Robert Collier letter book. North Charleston, SC: Createspace Independent Publishing Platform.

its benefits won't matter because there's zero relevance. An important thing to note is that this doesn't necessarily mean the problem doesn't exist. The person simply hasn't recognized they're being affected by it.

2. Problem Aware: **Prospect becomes aware they have a problem**

At this stage the person knows they have a problem, and they have at least a vague sense that your knowledge, products or services can help them solve it. Generally speaking, if someone has taken the time to subscribe to your email list, they're probably already at the "problem aware" stage.

This is good news, because the gap between "unaware" and "problem aware" is actually quite difficult to establish. For these reasons, the details for how to do this are outside the scope of this book. But broadly, when someone moves from unaware to problem aware, it means they've identified with a problem that's been introduced to them.

3. Solution Aware: **Prospect becomes aware a solution to their problem exists**

The bridge between Problem Awareness to Solution Awareness is likely where we'll intercept a new subscriber to our email list.

In a solution email, you provide value in the form of solutions to problems you know your subscribers are struggling with. By providing advice and expertise, your audience can come to recognize you as an authority with the experience and know-how to help them. As you send Solution Aware emails you educate, build rapport, and establish trust.

In 1972, Allen Newell and Herbert Simon published a book called *Human Problem Solving*.[57] Here, they outlined their theory of the *problem space*: the area where people search for solutions to a problem. According to the theory, a problem space consists of the current problem state, the goal state, as well as all the possible states in between.

---

[57] Newell, A. and Simon, H. A. (1971) Human Problem Solving. Harlow, England: Longman Higher Education.

What happens in the Solution Aware stage, is we help the subscriber fully establish their *problem space*. They become aware of the desired *goal state*, as well as any other possible states in between that might inhibit their process toward that goal. It's our job to show them the solutions so they can make their own way.

4. Product Aware: **Prospect becomes aware your product solves their problem**

The passage from Solution Aware to Product Aware is the realization that *your product* is what will most effectively take them towards their *goal state*. Your product should now be introduced as the tool they've been looking for to help them reach it.

If awareness has progressed successfully, then at this stage a product offer or promotion will rarely be seen as annoying. You'll be simply providing more value. In fact, if you've followed the stages correctly, you will never once have annoyed your subscriber. You'll have only ever been seen as providing massive value, always there to help provide advice and help with the problem they're grappling with.

This doesn't mean you're forcing anyone to buy. There's no hard selling. If your product isn't a good fit, that person isn't a customer — you're simply introducing your product to someone who likely needs it. It also doesn't mean you don't have to sell your product at all; you must still do the work of stating product benefits and tying them back to the problem. We must make it explicitly clear that your product bridges the gap between the current problem and the goal state, passing over the uncomfortable indeterminacy of the other possible states in between.

5. Most Aware: **Prospect becomes aware your product is the best solution**

The passage between Product Aware and Most Aware is subtle. This is where you reassure your subscriber that your product will take them to their goal state. They know what your product is and how it can help them. They're ready to buy, and these emails help you assuage final concerns to ultimately convert.

For subscribers who are Most Aware, they need concerns and questions addressed, security guaranteed or price adjusted. This is somewhat equivalent to the objection handling stage of the sales process. It's where conversion optimizations are implemented, with incentives such as discounts, bundles or guarantees now taking center stage in your messaging strategy.

The Curation Advantage

To recap: The goal of the Dispersal stage is to build *engagement*. By doing this, you create a strong foundation for further advanced techniques and avoid the risk of the top-down collapse early on. The means of building that engagement is through sending timely and relevant emails that always provide value.

The *Five Awareness States* make it much easier to ensure your emails are timely and relevant. By organizing your audience into these groupings, you'll understand what emails you need to send to whom, what exactly needs to be said to each segment, and what you need to do in order to progress the lower states (Problem Aware, Solution Aware) towards the higher states (Product Aware, Most Aware).

At the lower end of the scale you focus on education, developing a subscriber into a customer. At the higher end of the scale, you can then speak directly about your products and their benefits, knowing with a good degree of certainty they'll be warmly received.

In this context, sending a promotional offer to a contact who is only "Problem Aware" is like proposing on the first date. Too much, too soon. The work of drawing attention to the problem hasn't been done yet, so it's not realistic to expect this individual to have yet made the connection between your product and its value to them personally. The product and its benefits aren't yet relevant.

When someone subscribes to your list, they've opened a direct line of communication. Using the *Five Awareness States*, this direct line uniquely allows you to nurture and develop a subscriber across all stages of awareness.

This is one of the great features unique to email marketing. Remember, email is the only communication channel on the internet that you completely control. No algorithm changes, no policy updates, no platform risk - and potentially fully automated. This is part of the reason terms such as "inbound" and "funnels" are almost synonymous with email. Just try progressing and tracking a potential customer's Awareness State on a platform like Facebook or Instagram. It will be very difficult, if you're able to pull it off at all.

But this direct line of communication isn't just helpful for improving engagement and pathing the way to conversions. It's at the core of what makes a Walled Garden successful.

In the previous chapter, we covered how the strategy of the Walled Garden is to control *the distribution* of information to a market over which they have privileged access. This distribution is only attained by first amassing an audience of users, which they attract by offering the best possible user experience.[58] It's precisely this *best possible user experience* offered by these companies that allows them to be like *sources*, rather than *sinks*. I call it the *Curation Advantage*.

For most of human history, an individual did not encounter that much new information over their lifetime. The arrival of the internet has fundamentally changed this. The average person has gone from having access to only the information inside the books within their house or local library, to nearly all human knowledge. As author Taylor Pearson described it in his book *The End of Jobs*, "*Everyone now has access to the sum total of human knowledge and resources at their fingertips, 24 hours a day, 7 days a week, 365 days a year*".[59]

As we have gradually transformed into, via author James Gleick, "*creatures of information*",[60] it's ironic this reality is most easily described to us,

---

[58] Stratechery.com. Defining Aggregators – Stratechery by Ben Thompson [ONLINE] Available at: https://stratechery.com/2017/defining-aggregators/

[59] Pearson, T. (2015) The end of jobs: Money, meaning and freedom without the 9-to-5. Three Magnolia.

[60] Gleick, J. (2011) The information: A history, a theory, a flood. New York, NY: Pantheon Books.

again, in terms of data: A 2014 International Data Corporation (IDC) study predicted that *"By 2020, about 1.7 megabytes of new information will be created every second for every human being on the planet and the accumulated digital universe of data will grow from 4.4 zettabytes today to around 44 zettabytes or 44 trillion gigabytes"*.[61]

That prediction has turned out to be correct, with a follow up 2017 paper *Data Age 2025* again predicting that *"the Global Datasphere will grow from 33 zettabytes in 2018 to 175 zettabytes by 2025"*.[62] The paper attempts to describe the magnitude of this much data: *"If you were to store 175 zettabytes on DVDs, your stack of DVDs would be long enough to circle Earth 222 times"*.

It was fitting then when information theorist Peter Lyman concluded somewhat defeatedly in a 2003 report: *"It is clear that we are all drowning in a sea of information"*.[63] But what has caused such a massive deluge of information over the last two decades? The answer is *digitization*. Everything that was previously analog is now being scanned, copied, uploaded and transformed into bits. Books, documents, records, artworks. Almost nothing has been left untouched. In our mission to digitize everything around us, we've unlocked vast amounts of information that was previously inaccessible. The Walled Gardens are perfect examples of this.

When we looked at the examples of Uber and Airbnb, we saw that they commoditized the supply side of their respective markets, taxis and hotels. The way they did this was by focusing on previously hidden assets - underused cars and spare rooms, respectively.

But the more accurate description of the service these companies provide is in how they provide access to this abundance of newly digitized information. It's the sheer volume which calls for, again via Gleick, the

---

[61] Pwc.com. Data the new Smart [ONLINE] Available at: https://www.pwc.com/ng/en/assets/pdf/data-the-new-smart.pdf

[62] Bernardmarr.com. How Much Data Is There In the World? | Bernard Marr [ONLINE] Available at: https://bernardmarr.com/how-much-data-is-there-in-the-world/

[63] Peter Lyman, Hal R. Varian, et al (2000) "How Much Information?" Available at: https://groups.ischool.berkeley.edu/archive/how-much-info/how-much-info.pdf.

increasingly essential service of *"filtering and searching"*. Helping users search through the glut of information has proved to be extremely valuable, as the now two trillion dollar valued Google might attest.[64] This is what forms the essence of *the Curation Advantage*.

So Uber filtered and curated the new digital over-abundance of underused privately owned vehicles, and Airbnb did the same for a new digital over-abundance of empty rooms and unused apartments. The way they both captured user attention was by then acting as the middle-men, brokering between this newly curated information and the audience who could benefit from it.

Facebook, in a way, also filtered and curated newly digitized information that was previously embedded in our individual social lives. The platform then provided a curatory experience of these events within our individual "social networks".

When this information became digitized, it became overabundant. The supply side of the market became commoditized. Filtering and curating this information then becomes one of the basic and most valuable services one can offer: creating order from chaos. With this in mind,we too must focus on providing a great customer experience above all else — from the very first impression to the hundredth purchase.

The Five Awareness States allows us to make sure that the information we're sharing with our subscribers is always relevant and timely. When you don't have strong engagement, it simply means that the information you're sharing with your audience isn't relevant – ; you've failed to effectively curate. But when we share timely and relevant information, we are leveraging *the Curation Advantage* that has helped to build the multi-billion dollar companies of the past decade. All we need to do is guide our subscribers through the surfeit of information that pollutes their lives.

Knowing all this, how do we actually apply lessons of the Five Awareness States? How can we make sure we're best leveraging *the Curation Advantage*?

---

[64] Theverge.com. Google's parent company briefly hits $2 trillion valuation - The Verge [ONLINE] Available at: https://www.theverge.com/2021/11/8/22770569/alphabet-google-market-cap-hits-2-trillion

The Awareness Automation

The following will walk through the first automation we'll build as part of the *Natural Orders* system. One of the biggest mistakes people make (myself included when I first started out), is to put on the "auteur architect" hat and start penciling out a masterpiece email automation strategy from scratch. From my experience, this is always the wrong way to go about it.

Just like a natural ecosystem, complexity is never planned, but emerges. As Gall's Law states, *"A complex system that works is invariably found to have evolved from a simple system that worked"*. As we've addressed with the top-down cascade, ideal conditions can only develop by provision of a strong foundation.

So I always recommend those just getting started with email marketing and automation to *keep it simple*. Instead of planning a masterpiece funnel from scratch, it's always better to start with good fundamentals and add pieces from there as they make sense. For many store owners exploring email marketing and automation for the first time, building a simple foundational strategy that I call the *Awareness Automation* is the best place to start. It nurtures your new subscribers and makes them more likely to become buyers, as we've covered, but it also provides some other huge benefits. Specifically, it:

- **Resurrects your old blog articles, social media posts and emails.**
  All that old content you spent ages creating? This can finally be reused to repeatedly add value, seen anew by every new subscriber you add. By setting up an Awareness Automation, you'll breathe new life into your old content.

  Automated emails will allow you to share your valuable existing content with every new subscriber. This will communicate a strong narrative about your brand, provide value, build engagement and of course progress the stage of awareness.

- **Keeps your engagement high and your list healthier than it's ever been.**
  By ensuring each new subscriber is receiving only valuable content upfront, you'll be building a great first impression that establishes a behavioral feedback loop to engage. This will skyrocket your engagement.

  People sometimes don't believe me when I tell them that you can sometimes achieve open rates of 35-45% for this sequence, but that's the goal. The whole point is not to tank your engagement with irrelevant emails and always provide value.

- **Identifies and automatically sends offers to subscribers when they're ready to receive them.**
  The Awareness Automation automatically sends relevant offers when your subscribers are product aware — when they're most ready to receive them.

  While we'll build on the conversion of subscribers into customers in the next chapter, even with the Awareness Automation you can expect conversions to start occurring as subscribers are nurtured to the point where buying makes sense.

- **Allows nearly endless scope and customization.**
  The Awareness Automation is built with expansion in mind. After setting up an Awareness Automation you can theoretically take your automation strategy in any direction you want, confident your foundations are strong with a sequence that forms a solid ecosystem base.

- **Gathers engagement metrics and enables you to make data-driven decisions.**
  There are few better ways to gather conversion and engagement metrics, and fewer again that build stores of that data automatically over time. This will be valuable in the following chapters, but for now it's the first step towards making decisions based on more than just intuition.

How the Awareness Automation Works

Let's first look at an overview of how the Awareness Automation works, then dive into each part in a bit more detail. What I'll outline here is a basic guide that you can use to apply the principles of the Awareness Automation, no matter what EMS you use, from the most simple to highly advanced.

With this in mind, you can be creative about how you apply it to your business. For example, the exact conditions that represent a progression of awareness ("last five emails", etc.) matters far less than the central heuristic of only sending to subscribers you are certain have exhibited strong engagement before specifically trying to sell them products.

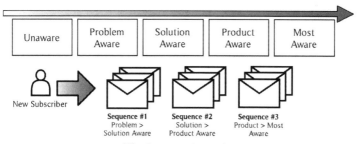

The Awareness Automation

Use the following guide, as with all others throughout this book, as general strategies within a broader useful framework. This way, you'll be more creative in how you apply it to your unique situation and avoid myopically copying what is a necessarily simplified system. Below is an idealized awareness automation that can be used to progress new subscribers through the stages of awareness.

The Awareness Automation is made up of three main sequences you'll build inside your email marketing software (EMS):

Sequence 1. Problem Aware > Solution Aware
Goal: Introduce the Problem Concept.

Sequence 2. Solution Aware > Product Aware

Goal: Introduce the Goal State.

Sequence 3. Product Aware > Most Aware
Goal: Conversion.

Immediately after a new subscriber is added to your list, they'll be placed into the first of these, which is nothing more than a series of five to fifteen emails (depending on how much content you have available), with each email delivering just a single piece of content.

How do you know when a subscriber has successfully progressed between each stage? It's simply a condition based on engagement. In Sequence 1 the subscriber will eventually be sent all of the emails within it. At the very end of the sequence, all we need to do is add a condition that checks: "has this subscriber interacted with any of the past five emails?".

It will be either yes or no. If yes, we can confidently say they've been engaging with our content and in turn have been exposed to a series of problems and solutions. If no, this person has low engagement and we should reduce our sending frequency by filtering them out.

So most subscribers will receive both Sequence 1 and 2. But only subscribers showing strong engagement will be graduated to the final Product Aware Sequence 3. The reason for this, is that including low engagements in the next sequence (Product Aware) is likely to hurt overall engagement — the foundation of your ecosystem.

That's really it. You have three sequences of emails arranged according to the States of Awareness, and you use conditions to filter out subscribers who don't engage.

Designing Intentional Feedback Loops

Part of the reason the Awareness Automation is so effective is because it intentionally creates a feedback loop where engagement is encouraged.

The Hooked Model. Credit: Nir Eyal

In his book *Hooked: How to Build Habit Forming Products*[65], author and behavioral designer Nir Eyal describes a feedback loop that helps software companies establish user behaviors which compound into beneficial outcomes. Although conceived for the reinforcement of behaviors in the context of software products, this mechanism can also be applied to your email database.

Eyal's feedback loop, *The Hooked Model*, has four stages:

1. **A Trigger**: Beginning with an external motivation from the product, a user is driven to take a first action.

2. **An Action**: After being prompted by the external trigger, the action is performed successfully.

3. **A Variable Reward**: In response to successful action, a user is given a "variable" reward.

4. **User Investment:** The above variability is an element of novelty. By making the exact reward for an action unknowable in advance, it develops user interest in continuing to take the action. This investment leads to an internally motivated trigger (rather than the initial external one), and the user becomes invested in taking further action on their own.

A simple example of the Hooked Model in action is Facebook's notification system. After becoming a user, Facebook hits you with an initial notification. You head to the app and select the bright red notification icon which takes you to whatever has happened in your social network.

---

[65] Eyal, N. (2014) Hooked: How to build habit-forming products. London, England: Portfolio Penguin.

The variable reward then kicks in: was the result something boring? Or was it exciting like someone commenting on or liking a picture you just posted? The variability of this reward creates user investment.

Next time you get a notification, you're much more likely to click on it in order to see what type of reward is in store: will it be boring or exciting? Over time, you won't need to be prompted to log back onto Facebook. In fact, many people refresh their Facebook newsfeed dozens of times a day to see what new notifications are waiting for them.

When designed thoughtfully, the Dispersal Stage also does this to an extent. We can incorporate each of the Hooked stages into the way new subscribers experience their first interactions with your brand's emails.

An email from a new brand in a subscriber's inbox is novel and interesting. This is the reason "Welcome" emails have famously high open rates (at around ~50% industry-wide).[66] The newness is novel, but it very quickly wears off. By using this novel interest as a chance to provide value with your very first impression, you provide a reward for that initial opening. From that point on, consistent value in your emails results in them standing out and being more likely to be opened in future.

The Problem with Engagement Metrics

There is one problem with engagement metrics that is worth noting. Most email clients use in-built spam detection measures which automatically trigger opens (and sometimes clicks)[67] as they scan messages coming into the Inbox. What this means is that it's becoming increasingly unreliable to track the traditional engagement metrics of Open and Click rates.

This has been accelerated by recent changes by Apple, who in a June 2021 press release announced a new suite of privacy changes to their

---

[66] MarketingSherpa. Welcome Messages Get Highest Open Rates of All Email Campaigns: How to Improve Yours | MarketingSherpa [ONLINE] Available at: https://www.marketingsherpa.com/article/how-to/how-to-improve-yours

[67] Createandsell.co. Yesterday, Apple obliterated email open tracking - Create & Sell [ONLINE] Available at: https://createandsell.co/issues/apple-block-open-tracking

proprietary email client, Mail. In the statement, Apple announces the new feature they dub Mail Privacy Protection, which *"... helps users prevent senders from knowing when they open an email and masks their IP address so it can't be linked to other online activity or used to determine their location."* [68]

The privacy debate fuelling these changes is multifaceted with strong points on both sides. Yet the important thing to understand is that despite changes by individual email clients, the reliability of these metrics has been on a downward trend for years. In fact, your current numbers for opens and clicks are likely already misleading or somewhat inaccurate.

So what's the solution? How do we properly measure engagement going forward?

The most reliable solution I've found is to look at the actions subscribers take *from* your emails rather than their actual engagement with the email itself. This is a much more reliable indicator of how effective a marketing message has been. In fact, as one recent experiment discovered, opens and clicks can actually be poor measures of engagement especially if not seen in light of broader business goals.[69] This reflects my own experience, and is why I recommend that instead of relying on opens and clicks to determine engagement, instead focus on the following:

- **Keep Unsubscribes Low**: Instead of aiming for >30% opens, optimize for <0.5% unsubscribes.

- **Track CTA Completions**: Instead of aiming for >7% clicks, optimize for the number of results generated from the CTA (form fills, cart adds, enquiries, etc.).

---

[68] Apple.com. Apple advances its privacy leadership with iOS 15, iPadOS 15, macOS Monterey, and watchOS 8 - Apple [ONLINE] Available at: https://www.apple.com/newsroom/2021/06/apple-advances-its-privacy-leadership-with-ios-15-ipados-15-macos-monterey-and-watchos-8/

[69] Gon.to. You're Measuring Your Email Nurtures Effectiveness Wrong [ONLINE] Available at: https://gon.to/2017/01/25/you-re-measuring-your-email-nurtures-effectiveness-wrong/

It's important to note that Opens and Clicks aren't useless. Even if your EMS tells you that you get 30% open rates on average, the number itself isn't as important as the fluctuations from this point. For example, if you notice in three months that this average has decreased to around 20%, it's still a safe bet to say your engagement has decreased.

There is a reason I recommend using them for the Dispersal stage: they are still a helpful method for tracking engagement over time. The measurement itself won't be accurate but its movement can still be a lagging indicator for declines in engagement and overall list health.

Planning your Awareness Automation

So with a broad overview of how the system works, how does one actually build it? It's easy to talk about these different stages and what they mean. It's easier still for me to tell you that you need to send content that represents each stage. But in practice, progressing between each stage smoothly is much easier said than done. You can't simply send email after email of "value" hoping that it also progresses a subscriber.

The first step for building an Awareness Automation is some planning. You need a solid understanding of your brand's value proposition, who your target customers are, and what existing content you have at your disposal. In other words, you must have the fundamental knowledge and background research of your market that would typically be required to write effective copy.

Along with that, take the following steps to prepare building an *Awareness Automation*:

Step 1. Gather your previously published blog articles, social media posts, videos and emails.

All your content from site copy to blog posts to whitepapers. Choose content with an emphasis on those that aren't simply trying to sell products. These are rarer than you might think and you'll need all of them for the earlier awareness states.

Step 2. Refer back to the Five Awareness States and arrange your content to fit beneath the stages Problem, Solution and Product Aware.

Refer to the explanation earlier in this chapter to see where they fit best.

Step 3. Beginning with your Problem Aware content, outline the sequence of your Awareness Automation.

There will be one email per unique piece of content. Line up each email in the order you plan to send them based on your arrangement in Step 2.

This is the hard part. While the structure is deceptively simple, the way you construct your Awareness Automation requires a bit of thought because it will play a large part in determining the brand experience for new subscribers, and that's a topic with enough depth for a book of its own. It's worth setting aside a decent amount of time to think through this, as every new subscriber will be receiving this same brand experience.

So make it powerful. Pay attention to the narrative you're creating with each email; what you're saying about your brand; and especially what *world* you're building for your subscribers. A subscriber must first buy into your brand's universe — the possible future identity it represents to them — *before* they'll buy your products.

Building your Awareness Automation

Part of the beauty of the Awareness Automation is you only need very basic features to pull it off. In its most basic form, it's really just a string of emails with some quite basic segmentation conditions.

Each EMS is slightly different. But even the free plan of the most entry-level EMS is usually enough to set this up (which is great as it allows beginners to experience the massive ROI these sequences yield, with little to no extra commitment or software migration headaches).

Individually, each of these emails are very simple. The subject line is related to the content you're sharing. When the subscriber opens the email there is a brief description of the article with a call-to-action (CTA) to read the content.

This content can be anything from an existing blog article or social media post, or repurposed copy from your site, for example. The point is, each email is meant to loop your email subscriber back onto your social media account, website, blog, or other platform where you regularly share content.

With this in mind, these guidelines should help you figure out how it should all look when you're finished:

1. Begin with a Welcome email

Immediately after you add a new subscriber, send them a Welcome email. Here you'll briefly give an introduction to the problems you'll be helping your subscribers solve.

Welcome emails are very high engagement by nature, but definitely don't be tempted to add an ask just yet. Instead, use the Welcome as an opportunity to make a great first impression. Introduce yourself (but keep it brief) and try to offer something you're certain will be valuable upfront.

Keep in mind the importance of feedback loops: this is an opportunity to set expectations on the value you aim to provide in coming emails.

2. Create your Problem Aware emails

Write a short description for each email, and include a clear call-to-action that links to the blog post, video, etc. Write a short description that connects your content to the problem you're helping your subscriber identify. Include around 3-6 of these.

For the first sequence, a typical Problem Aware email might look like:

Subject: **How to Tell if You're X**
Message: Introductory text either pulled from the article or written to draw subscriber interest.
CTA: **[Click here to read How to Tell if You're X]**
---

3. Create a dedicated "narrative" email

If you have a well written "About" page on your site, this is a great way to repurpose it.

The goal of this email is to establish not only that you understand what the problem of your subscriber is (which you've already proven by linking useful content), but also what you're all about, and how you're uniquely poised to help solve it.

It also pre-frames the next section of emails, so subscribers can better understand the personality behind the authority you're trying to establish.

4. Create your Solution Aware emails

Write a short description for each email and include a clear call-to-action that links to the blog post, video, etc. Write a short description that demonstrates how the content helps to solve the problem. Include around 3-6 of these.

For the second sequence, not much changes in terms of email structure. You merely arrange your content by virtue of either introducing problem concepts or introducing goal state concepts.

For the second sequence, a typical Solution Aware email might look like:

Subject: **5 Ways to Solve X**
Message: Introductory text either pulled from the article or written to draw subscriber interest.
CTA: **[Click here to read 5 Ways to Solve X]**

One to three times per week, a new piece of this content is sent to the new subscriber. Make sure you have at least two days (for shorter content) and up to a full week (for longer and more in- depth content) between each email.

This may seem a bit contrarian: common advice urges more email equals more sales. But this only applies to Product Aware or Fully Aware subscribers who are already considering purchasing. Sending too many emails to subscribers too early will cause overwhelm, leading to disinterest, leading to poor engagement and unnecessarily increased unsubscribes.

So, it's better to start off slowly. Once your subscriber has reached Product Awareness, frequency can then be increased.

5. Create your Product Aware emails

For Product Aware emails, make sure your content describes the benefits of your product. (This is a good place to repurpose promotional and sales material for your product).

Alternatively, if lacking promotional benefit-driven content, start by linking directly to the sales page for the product. In any case, make sure at least one email links directly to an opportunity to purchase. Include around 3-4 of these. Increase sending frequency for Product Aware subscribers, optimizing for more emails with high engagement and low unsubscribes.

So to recap, the Awareness Automation is designed to help you get started with automation in the simplest way possible. It's also the easiest way to automate sending emails to your subscribers in a way that:

- Consistently adds value, not asks.
- Builds strong engagement.
- Reduces unsubscribes.
- Builds trust with your subscribers.
- Progresses audience awareness so they're more likely to buy.
- Collates and collects conversion metric data for better decisions.
- Repurposes your old content you spent hours making.
- All the while guaranteeing more sales than any non-automation alternative.

This checks all the boxes necessary in building a strong foundation for more advanced automation.

Segmentation and Personalization

The Awareness Automation we built above is just a simple string of emails. This works well as a foundation for the reasons we covered, but one under-addressed point is the amount of data that this automation will also gather about your subscribers.

What we've demonstrated in the Awareness Automation, in its most basic form, is the power of segmentation of personalization. This is an important feature at the heart of what makes email marketing automation so valuable to your business.

By setting up the Awareness Automation, we've taken the first steps from having just an email address, to collecting data for a detailed customer profile. We started this by focusing on collecting data for one metric: engagement. We now have a system that automatically tracks which subscriber opens or clicks which emails, and from that we can infer what's relevant to them.

Why is this important? With personalization, you are using one of the most powerful tools available for increasing sales. Your subscriber's engagement with previous emails determines which emails they'll receive next. This is *personalization*: building a highly segmented customer journey unique for every individual subscriber. As we'll cover in the next section, this improves conversions dramatically.

In the next chapter, we'll go much deeper into what makes the Product Aware subscribers convert. We'll double down our focus on the power of segmentation and personalization and build the next natural progression of our ecosystem: the *Recruitment Stage*.

Summary

- **The Golden Rule of Email Marketing is to always provide value: *educate, inspire or entertain*.** We need to maintain strong engagement, so must avoid spamming our audience.

- **The best way to make sure you are always following the Golden Rule is by knowing your audience's Stage of Awareness.** Eugene Schwartz's *Five Awareness States* is a commonly used and powerful model allowing you to reliably group your subscribers by what information will be most valuable to them.

- **The Awareness Automation is at the heart of the Dispersal stage.** Use the *Five Awareness States* as a framework for nurturing your leads. It reuses your existing content to educate, inspire or entertain your audience while also progressing them through the 5 Stages.

- **The Product Aware stage should be separated from the main sequence.** Only those who show engagement with Problem Aware and Solution Aware emails receive promotional information. This way you avoid spam and add greater personalization.

I.Dispersal

The Mountain Ash (*Eucalyptus regnans*) forms the canopy of a temperate rainforest in South-Eastern Australia. Mt Field National Park, Tasmania.
Credit: Chrmichel

II.
RECRUITMENT

The Mountain Ash (*Eucalyptus regnans*) is the tallest flowering plant in the world. It's also among the tallest of any tree species, with individuals in its native habitat of South-Eastern Australia sometimes exceeding heights of 100 meters (~330 feet). That's as tall as a 30-story building.

The Mountain Ash, while a very large tree, reaches just shy of the heights achieved by its North American neighbors, the California Coast Redwoods (*Sequoia sempervirens*) — known to be the tallest trees in the world. Apart from sharing similarly impressive stature, these two species also share prestigious names for their tallest individuals.

In Australia the state of Tasmania's tallest Mountain Ash *Centurion* measures in at 100.5m, and the nearby *Icarus Dream* is reported to have achieved a height of 98.8m. But these just barely lose out to the even taller (and again suitably named) Coast Redwoods, with Northern California's giant *Hyperion* measuring in at a massive 115.85m - the tallest tree in the world - followed closely by its slightly shorter brothers *Helios* and *Icarus,* all three sharing residence in the *Redwood National and State Parks.*

So the Mountain Ash are big trees, by any standard. They're also important enough to have been granted names like *Centurion*. Why then, in 1984, did a team of Australian scientists deliberately light a wildfire to burn down a grove of mature Mountain Ash, right outside the country's capital? For such a magnificent tree, standing amongst some of the tallest on the planet (and which are, according to this study, "*relatively fire-sensitive*"), surely there must have been a suitably important reason for their destruction?

It turns out that by burning the Mountain Ash, the scientists conducting the study knew the fire would cause the tree to drop hundreds of new seeds. "*Relatively fire-sensitive*", yes: members of the *Eucalyptus* genus have actually evolved to incorporate fire into their lifecycle. Burn-off events such as the one in the study, rather than destroying the tree, actually help to facilitate new growth by triggering the dispersal of seeds.

The study then tracked what happened to those seeds, and what factors were influencing their survival in the burned area and adjacent environment.[70] More broadly, the scientists were seeking to better understand the mechanics behind a process in Ecology known as *Recruitment*.

Recruitment

Recruitment describes the point at which an organism from one environment becomes part of a new one. It's easier to explain with a specific example. The Mountain Ash happen to be a good vehicle for this. It's straightforward to define when a tree has been "recruited". All the scientists must do is set a benchmark height. Any new saplings that reach that size are counted as new members of the existing community. All those who die before reaching the target size are excluded — they've failed to "recruit". In this particular study, with a clear definition of success given for Recruitment, the scientists were then able to look at all the factors that influenced it.

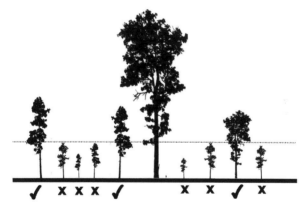

A successfully "recruited" tree is defined as having reached a certain height benchmark.

---

[70] Dennis J. O'Dowd and A. Malcolm Gill (0108/1984) "Predator Satiation and Site Alteration Following Fire: Mass Reproduction of Alpine Ash (Eucalyptus Delegatensis) in Southeastern Australia," Ecology, 65(4), pp. 1052–1066.

In an email marketing context, we set our own benchmark to define successful Recruitment. After *Dispersing* into our ecosystem, who would we determine whether that individual has been *recruited*? The answer is conversion. With a long-term view for our ecosystem to turn subscribers into customers, a recruit in our context is any subscriber who achieves that crucial first sale. This chapter will walk through how to do that.

STAGE	FOUNDATION	DISPERSAL	RECRUITMENT	ESTABLISHMENT
GOAL	TSC	Engagement	Conversion	Lifetime Value
METHOD	Improve Optin Placements	Provide Value Progress Awareness	Personalization	Increase New Orders Increase Repeat Orders Increase Average Order Value
AUTOMATIONS	N/A	Awareness Automation	Semantic Automation	LTV Automation

Conversion

In the Dispersal stage, the focus was on building the foundations for an email ecosystem our new subscribers wouldn't want to leave. By making sure our emails were timely and relevant, we improved our engagement and made it less likely our subscribers would get bored and leave.

But the The *Awareness Automation* we built in the previous chapter doesn't focus on getting our subscribers to buy. While it can yield conversions on its own, it's not built to specifically optimize for this — its focus is engagement. So referring back to the stages of succession, having only an *Awareness Automation* is something like having an ecosystem consisting of just some grass and shrubs. It's better than bare rocks and lichen, sure. But when you could potentially have a thriving rainforest, it's not living up to its potential. So we need something dedicated to taking our nascent ecosystem across to the next stage.

This is why in the Recruitment stage, having laid strong foundations, we want to now help optimize our subscribers convert, or "recruit", into paying customers. To do this we'll build a set of sequences designed to collect data about our subscribers. These will come together into a system that monitors interactions, segments subscribers into their interest areas, then sends targeted emails to those segments, all automatically. These targeted emails are really what is meant when we talk about "personalization" in email marketing.

Personalization

One of the big advantages email has over other platforms is that we can segment and divide our database any way we wish. Knowing this, instead of sending the same email to everyone, we should seek to send the most valuable email we can to each person.

This is the real reason why email is able to generate so much ROI compared to other channels. As described in *Dispersal*, it's these two factors that determine the difference between an email being perceived as spam or value. An email with great timing and relevance is not only much more likely to get opened and not result in an unsubscribe — it's also much more likely to lead to a purchase.

A fifteen percent discount on an irrelevant product is spam. Similarly, a well-designed solution to a problem your subscriber isn't experiencing also has zero value to them. On the other hand, an offer that solves an immediate problem has a lot of value. How much you're willing to pay for a bottle of water will depend on how thirsty you are. If your customer is ready to hear about your offer, the chances are much greater they'll actually convert.

So in general, a great offer with poor timing and low relevance will convert more poorly than a mediocre offer sent with perfect timing. This means personalizing your emails is really just about improving their timing and relevance. By making sure every email we send to a subscriber is "personalized", we are really just making sure they're getting the most relevant content sent to them at the right time.

With this in mind, how can we possibly know who should get sent what, and when? The Five Awareness States we used in the Dispersal stage are a great place to start. But when we know someone is ready to purchase, we need to have more information. What product exactly are they interested in? What category of products? We need to have a clear picture of who our subscribers are. We need to get a clearer understanding of their needs, wants and behaviors. This is a big problem in marketing, but it's one that email automation can help solve.

The Black Box Problem

A Black Box is any system where there is a clear input and an output, but the factors that produce that output are unknowable. You don't know what's going on inside of it.

Nature is a good example of a Black Box System. Ecologists have a decent grasp of cause-and-effect factors in ecosystems.[71] Consider the experiment at the beginning of the chapter: the scientists knew what the resulting process would be (dispersal), and they were confident about how they could get it started (a fire). Scientists understand what processes take place, and what they generally result in — but how exactly do they work? What happens in the middle? How precisely do the inputs lead to the outputs?

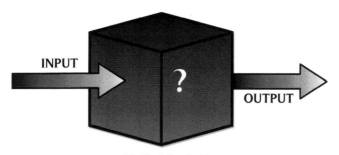

The Black Box Problem

Only by focusing on the black box — what happens in the middle of the *Black Box* — could they progress their understanding. It turns out this is the most difficult information to uncover.It's the same problem we face in our own email marketing ecosystem. We know that we send

---

[71] Mittelbach, G. G. and McGill, B. J. (2019) Community Ecology. 2nd ed. London, England: Oxford University Press.

an email and a certain number of people open and click on the offer (the input). We also know that a certain percentage of those people will purchase (the output). But what about the middle? What *really* determines whether or not they buy?

Opening the Black Box

Marketing Professor Philip Kotler actually applied the idea of the Black Box to marketing in his book *Marketing Management*.[72] In Kotler's model, he groups all possible information about a buyer into three categories:

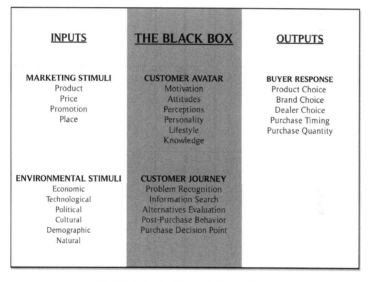

The Black Box Problem applied to marketing.

Let's look at these three categories in more detail:

---

[72] Kotler, P. (1991) Marketing Management: Analysis, Planning, Implementation and Control. 7th ed. London, England: Prentice-Hall.

1. **Inputs**: The *Marketing Stimuli* are the factors we use to build a campaign strategy, sometimes referred to as the classic "four P's" of marketing. The *Environmental Stimuli* are the market conditions we pay attention to when creating that strategy.

2. **Outputs**: In this category, the *Buyer's Responses* are usually straightforward to find out. We can usually find out information about what someone bought: for example what product, how much of it, who from and when.

3. **The Black Box**: But as I'll demonstrate, the most impactful information we can learn about our buyers is in the center. The factors of the Black Box are those that are typically the hardest to uncover. These include:

   a. **Customer Avatar**: This is everything we can know about an individual, or the ideal customer profile: Motivation, Attitudes, Perceptions, Personality, Lifestyle, Knowledge.

   a. **Customer Journey**: This includes all the stages a customer goes through to arrive at the purchase decision: Problem Recognition, Information Search, Alternatives Evaluation, Post-Purchase Behavior, Purchase Decision Point.

The Recruitment stage, then, is about setting up a system which helps to reveal more about these two categories. The data collected in the Dispersal stage is helpful, but it's incomplete. When we send an email in the Dispersal stage, our efforts in tracking *engagement* metrics are great for helping us set a strong foundation.

But for improving conversions, it's more important to understand those factors at the center of the Black Box. This is really nothing new: since the inception of marketing as a discipline, the number one determinant of success has been understanding your market. When we achieve deeper insight into our customers, and use this to create more timely and relevant offers, improving conversions.

The advantage Kotler's model provides is it shows us *precisely* where to construct our data collecting automations. Let's take a closer look at exactly how we'll do this.

The Semantic Layer

After someone subscribes to your email list, their email address serves as the foundation for all further data collection. As they click, open and navigate across your site we gather more data, and what we learn about them quickly compounds.

But the problem with all this information is that there is so much of it. We need a way to tell what the important and revealing actions are — adding an item to a shopping cart, or browsing within a certain category of products or services. First defining and then organizing this information necessitates what I refer to as *the Semantic Layer*.

The name sounds a bit abstract, but it's really very simple: it's simply a description given to a certain action. It's also very simple to implement. Every good EMS allows you to add additional information about individual subscribers through the use of what are often called "Tags" or sometimes "Custom Fields". These are short descriptive labels that can be attached to an email address in your database. It's a very simple, but very powerful feature that gives us a lot of control over how we manage things.

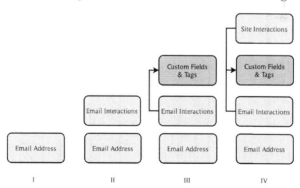

The Semantic Layer: Stages of Customer Data Aggregation

The Semantic Layer allows us to go from a single basic piece of data (an email address), into a complex profile about a person consisting of specific actions they have (or haven't) taken. It's in using this additional data that we can then segment and personalize the offers we send. The below image shows how just an email address can slowly be built into a high-information profile about a a customer:

Stage I: The process all starts with an email address — the new entrant to our ecosystem. When we set up the *Awareness Automation* in the Dispersal stage, we built an environment where this email address is less likely to unsubscribe or ignore our emails.

Stage II: As part of that *Awareness Automation*, every email we sent tracked when a subscriber interacted with it: opens, clicks, unsubscribes, spam complaints, etc. This actually serves our first stage of data collection: *Email Interactions*. Now you have an email address associated with certain actions, giving some basic insight into the interests of this individual. Already, it's much more than just an email address.

Stage III: This is where the Semantic Layer begins. Rather than being a catalog of interactions, this new layer we'll build *describes the meaning* of those interactions. In describing what a certain action *represents to us*, we sort our users into valuable segments. I'll give an example below.

Stage IV: In the final stage, we also collect events from outside the EMS. Now we can not only describe the meaning of interactions with emails we send, but the behaviors of our subscribers after they click a link from one of our emails. We can follow the interactions of a subscriber back to our site to see what products or services they show interest in, and again use the *Semantic Layer* to describe the meanings of those actions.

The point is that over time as we collect more data, this *Semantic Layer* becomes a source of great insight. We begin to open up the Black Box. As Kotler might describe, we will have data revealing both the *Customer Journey* (via engagement with certain emails and interactions on the site) and the *Customer Avatar* (via which offers are engaged with and what products they express interest in).

Crucially, this data opens up new creative and targeted marketing opportunities that wouldn't have been otherwise available. Using an eCommerce example:

- Subscriber A ignores an email you sent about shoes but opened and clicked links in the past five emails sent about shirts. Also, Subscriber A appears to be interested in Shirt A, as he has a tag that shows he has visited that product several times in a single browsing session. There are also 2000 other subscribers who have been given this same tag over the past two weeks.

- We can then make more interesting strategic decisions with this data. Should we send a dedicated campaign to all the subscribers with this tag? Is this a trend for this specific product that we should double down on? Should we build an automated sequence to target all those new subscribers being added to this tag?

Without *the Semantic Layer* you can't really get these insights - this information remains hidden inside the Black Box. But more importantly, without this information, you can't really do advanced email marketing automation at all. Because not only does *the Semantic Layer* provide the data necessary to make strategic decisions — it also serves as the central switchboard for your automation. It's what allows you to trigger and end sequences, segment and filter your subscribers, and generally ensure the right person is getting the right message at the right time.

A Tag Taxonomy

So far, this might still all seem a bit abstract. But setting up an effective *Semantic Layer* is actually quite simple. As mentioned, your EMS should already have all the tools you need to set it up through "tags" or "custom fields".

The problem is that most EMS typically provide very little instruction on how to get the most out of these features. Being simply an empty text field, they're very flexible, which is both a good and bad thing. While it offers you complete freedom in how you use them, without a proper plan in place you can quickly create a big mess. Without a strategy, you'll find one day your tags simply overwhelm you. Your subscribers will quickly gain a lot of different tags and you won't remember the function of any of them.

So you'll need a strategy for how you organize everything. Again, nature provides us with a solution.

Scientists long ago came up with a *taxonomy* to name, describe and classify the diversity of life. A taxonomy is simply an organized system for naming living things. But it's very powerful: with a naming structure that shares a common pattern, scientists from across the world can understand the relationships between different organisms, while also inferring their important characteristics.

For example, from just two words, "*sequoia sempervirens*", a scientist knows that the giant tree from the start of this chapter is related to all other trees that also start with the first word (the *genus*), *sequoia*. Because of the way the system is organized, they can then check to see that a *sequoia* is part of a *family* of organisms called *Cupressaceae*, the cypresses, which in turn is part of a broader *class* known as *Pinopsida*, or conifers.

Since they have knowledge of how the system is organized, these two Latin words carry a lot of meaning for those who know how the underlying system of naming works. By using a common *syntax* - a structured way of using words - we build relationships and importance for the things we apply them to. Without a proper taxonomy, it would be very hard to organize the approximately 1.2 million species of which we have current written knowledge. The information would be unstructured and naming organisms in Latin would quite literally be meaningless.

This is actually the best way to manage your own *Semantic Layer*. Mercifully, we don't need anything on the scale of the taxonomy of living organisms I described above. But it's pretty easy to come up with a taxonomy of your own. All you need to do is create some labels to describe the *sets* of information that appear frequently.

Here are some examples of tags using a proper tagging taxonomy:

- LEAD: 20% Discount Optin
  Applied to all subscribers who optin via a "20% discount" form on your site.

- STATUS: Unengaged
  Applied to all subscribers who haven't engaged with an email for 3 months.

- STAGE: Solution Aware
  Applied to all subscribers who interacted with an email in your Solution Aware sequence from the Dispersal stage.

- CUSTOMER: Campaign A
  Applied to all subscribers who purchased via a specific email – "Campaign A".

- PURCHASED: Black Shirt SKU11324
  Applied to all subscribers who purchased SKU11324.

Something like the above is what you're aiming for. It's kind of like the [*genus*]—[*species*] structure in *sequoia sempervirens*. For example, you can set it up so that every time someone subscribes to your list they get a tag with the starting syntax "LEAD". Similarly, the word "STATUS" can be put at the front of any tag where you deal with the management of that subscriber — unengaged, highly engaged, solution aware, etc.

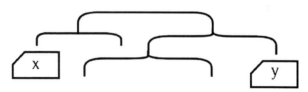

To access a free tag taxonomy planning document,
as well as other free resources that come with this book, please visit
symbiosgrowthautomation.com/natural-orders-resources

To recap: To improve our conversions we need to focus on personalization: and personalizing is really just about improving the *relevance* and *timing* of a given email.

The only way to do that is by understanding our customer. The Black Box and Kotler's *Customer Journey* and *Customer Avatar* guide us in knowing where to look to do so. To actually collect and organize this data we must build *the Semantic Layer*. We can then use this to segment, personalize, trigger automations and improve conversions.

The following section will give an overview of the mechanics underlying the engine of the Recruitment stage: what I call *the Semantic Automation*.

The Semantic Automation

With a broad understanding of *Semantic Layer* and the Black Box components, it's time to cover exactly how they work together. Taken in isolation these two concepts may seem unrelated. But in this section we'll reconcile them to show exactly how they work together.

1. **The first step is by getting clear on your *Customer Journey*:** By understanding what behaviors a subscriber takes on their way to purchase, you can remove any roadblocks that may be hindering that.

2. **Doing this will eventually reveal your *Customer Avatar*:** This clarity will reveal which actions are important to describe with the *Semantic Layer*. Over time this will lead to us learning more about our customers.

We'll use an eCommerce store as the example that follows. The reason for this is because in eCommerce, the *Customer Journey* tends to follow a pretty predictable formula: while details may vary slightly, in general a visitor browses the site, chooses a product they're interested in, adds it to their "cart", then goes to a "checkout" page where they complete their purchase.

For this reason, it's the most straightforward type of online business to use as an example. This doesn't mean you can't build the sequences of the Recruitment stage if you're not an eCommerce store. The broader concept applies whether you're a blog, software company or any other type of small online business looking to get the most out of email marketing and automation. You just need to make sure you have an understanding of your *Customer Journey* before you build the following sequences.

The Customer Journey in eCommerce

You may already be familiar with the idea of "Cart Abandonment". Put simply, an abandonment is a type of automation used in eCommerce that tracks when a visitor to a site has clicked the "Add to Cart" button for a product but has not followed through on their purchase. This sequence will then automatically trigger, sending one or more follow up emails that intercept the abandoning customer and save the conversion.

Cart Abandonment sequences are famously effective at improving conversion rates — but it's helpful to understand just how effective.

The amount of revenue loss that occurs due to customers adding items to carts and not completing the purchase is massive. eCommerce data science company Barilliance reported the average rate of Cart Abandonment in 2019 was ~77%.[73] This means more than three quarters of potential online retail sales in 2019 were lost due to customers deciding not to purchase, even after signaling strong interest in a product.

With Statista.com showing total 2019 online retail sales to be valued at roughly 3.5 billion US dollars, this means something in the range of 5-10 billion dollars of hypothetical online retail sales were lost that year — all of it added to an online cart (a strong signal of purchase intent if there ever was one) but never actually followed through.

While those are large figures in aggregate, the amount of potential lost sales for individual store owners is just as huge. Assuming a similar average Cart Abandonment rate of ~75%, an eCommerce store

---

[73] Barilliance.com, (2021). Complete List of Cart Abandonment Rate Statistics: 2006-2021 [ONLINE] Available at: https://www.barilliance.com/cart-abandonment-rate-statistics/#tab-con-7

with a yearly turnover of $1,000,000 would be missing out on around $3,000,000 of potential revenue just from abandoned carts alone.

So the numbers make it clear there's a large amount of revenue loss that can be avoided. And the way to avoid these losses has proven again and again to be via these email marketing abandonment sequences.

In fact, the effectiveness of Cart Abandonment email sequences is one of the most well-studied aspects of online retail and the results it yields are relatively consistent. Barilliance states in their 2020 email marketing statistics report that the average conversion from a Cart Abandonment email was 18.6%.[74] This means that, on average, one in every five Cart Abandonment emails you send will result in a conversion.

When applied to the above example of a store with a turnover of $1,000,000 and an abandonment-attributed loss of $3,000,000, this would represent $558,000 of recaptured additional yearly revenue from a single automated sequence.

Forms of Abandonment

The losses recaptured with these sequences are impressive and should be considered for that reason alone. But the more important and under-appreciated aspect is that they can also help reveal our *Customer Journey*.

The "Cart Abandonment" you are most likely familiar with is just one form of this sequence. It's actually part of a broader category of sequences, which I'll here refer to collectively as *Abandonment*. In fact, there are actually four main types of abandonment sequences:

1. Category Abandonment
2. Product Abandonment
3. Cart Abandonment
4. Checkout Abandonment

---

[74] Barilliance.com, (2021). 2021 Email Marketing ROI Statistics: Open Rate to Revenue [ONLINE] Available at: https://www.barilliance.com/email-marketing-statistics/

Together these four sequences will track the Customer Journey of a new subscriber — from exploring types of products (Category Abandonment), to selecting a specific product (Product Abandonment), to expressing discrete product interest (Cart Abandonment) all the way to final purchase objections (Checkout Abandonment).

Together, these sequences collect the data that allow you to personalize your emails. They are like cameras placed to take a snapshot at the parts of your store where the most critical actions take place. A camera at the category level, a camera at each product, and at the cart and checkout. You can then combine these individual snapshots with the engagement in your emails to take your *Semantic Layer* to a whole new level.

It's only by combining all four types of this sequence that we can get the data from all the stages of the *Customer Journey*, illuminate the *Customer Avatar*, and finally send targeted and personalized offers to our subscribers.

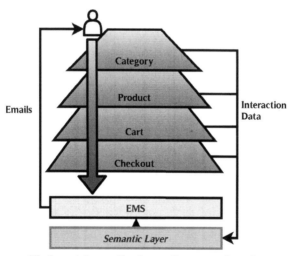

The Semantic Layer: Abandonment Sequences work together to reveal the Customer Journey.

These abandonment sequences are broken down into two broad categories, Purchase and Browse Abandonment:

1. Purchase Abandonment

The first sub-category of abandonment is concerned with retrieving lost sales. Let's look at these two sequences and how they work together to bridge the gap between different parts of the purchase process.

a. Cart Abandonment

The Cart Abandonment sequence is triggered when a prospect has viewed a product and added it to their cart but has left the site before they completed their purchase.

For many store owners, this sequence is their first taste of "marketing automation". It's also the most highly tested form of abandonment we'll look at here, with the stats I referred to above all referring specifically to this variant. The ROI is great, they're increasingly easy to set up, and they just about guarantee conversion increases for stores with moderate to high sales volume.

To quickly recap, a typical Cart Abandonment sequence looks something like:

1. A new visitor to your site finds a product they are interested in and clicks the "Add to Cart" button.
2. The product is added to the visitor's cart - usually visually indicated in the site banner.
3. The user then exits the site, without viewing their cart and completing their purchase.
4. If the visitor is an existing contact on your email database, this then triggers a Cart Abandonment sequence inside your EMS.
5. Around an hour or so later, the sequence sends an email to that visitor with the contents of their cart, with a call to action urging them to complete their purchase.
6. Often, one or two more reminder emails are sent to help improve conversion.

b. Checkout Abandonment

There is often confusion between Cart Abandonment and this second type, Checkout Abandonment. I often hear store owners referring to each of these interchangeably, which is an understandable confusion. The differences are subtle, but important.

While the former has shown interest in a product by adding it to their cart to be purchased, someone abandoning the checkout has added the product to their cart, and actually gone all the way towards making payment on that item, then stopped.

The difference between the two sounds small but there's a huge gap between flippantly adding something to your basket and actually taking steps to transact for that item.

Imagine going to the grocery store and picking something up from the shelf then realizing you don't need it and putting it back. That's similar to Cart Abandonment. Now imagine taking a cart full of items to the register, then walking away from your trolley when the cashier asks how you wish to pay. This is the equivalent of Checkout Abandonment.

Thinking about it in this way, the difference between purchase intention at either stage should be a bit clearer. The first example had a relatively weak intention in comparison to the second.

To illustrate further, Checkout Abandonment typically goes something like this:

1. A visitor to your site finds a product they are interested in and clicks the "Add to Cart" button.
2. The product is visually added to the visitor's cart - usually indicated somehow in the site banner.
3. *The visitor finishes browsing and then clicks their cart button to view their items.*
4. *Upon reviewing the items in their cart the visitor then clicks "Go to Checkout".*

5. *Now the checkout UX begins: prompts are given for transaction information such as name, address and card payment details.*
6. *The user then exits the site without having reached the stage of the checkout process that confirms their order and processes the transaction.*
7. If the visitor is an existing contact on your email database, this can then trigger a Checkout Abandonment sequence inside your EMS.
8. Around an hour or so later, the sequence sends an email to that visitor with the contents of their cart, with a call to action urging them to complete their purchase.
9. Often, one or two more reminder emails are sent to help improve conversion.

The difference between Cart and Checkout Abandonment can be seen in Steps 3-6 above. Checkout Abandonment can provide valuable data about your audience. You must uncover why they didn't go all the way to purchase: was the card declined? Did they realize they can't afford it? Thought better at the last minute? A link on the site enticed them away from completing the purchase? Solving these issues will invariably lead to better conversions and more revenue in the long term.

2. Browse Abandonment

While the above two forms of abandonment are concerned with improving conversions for those with an intention to purchase, the next two are slightly further from the sale. While the Cart and Checkout Abandonment sequences were concerned with retrieving lost sales, this second category of abandonment instead focuses on collecting the data about what a visitor is interested in so it can be used to personalize emails.

c. Product Abandonment

Product Abandonment tracks what products a site visitor views. Using this information, more targeted offers can be sent to those subscribers classed as Product Aware from the Dispersal stage. The strategy is to send increasingly targeted and personalized offers, thus improving the likelihood of conversion.

As opposed to a Cart or Checkout Abandonment sequence, a Product Abandonment plays out more like this:

1. A visitor to your site finds a product they are interested in but does not click the "Add to Cart" button.
2. There are then two potential triggers for a Product Abandonment:
   - Within the same browsing session, the visitor may return to view this product several more times.
   - Or, in one of these visits, the visitor may spend more than five minutes on the product page without navigating elsewhere.
3. The visitor then finishes browsing and exits the site.
4. If the visitor is an existing contact on your email database, the actions the visitor took on the site may be tracked.
   - Since the contact visited Product A more than x times in a single session, a tag "Product A" is added to the Semantic Layer.
   - Or, if the contact visited Product A and stayed on the page for more than five minutes, a tag "Product A" may be added to the Semantic Layer.

d. Category Abandonment

Zooming out further to our final type is Category Abandonment. Like Product Abandonment explored above, this sequence is also concerned with gathering visitor data to allow for more personalized offers. The mechanisms underlying both Category and Product Abandonment are very similar. However, it's important both are used in order to get the best snapshot of how visitors are interacting with your store.

The Category Abandonment sequence often looks something like this:

1. A visitor arrives at your site.
2. The visitor browses your store, and in doing so clicks on a specific category they are interested in: "Category B".
3. The visitor then finishes browsing and exits the site.

4. If the visitor is an existing contact on your email database, the actions the contact took on the site may be tracked.
    - Since the contact visited Category B in their session, a tag "Category B" is added to the Semantic Layer.

The biggest objection I usually hear from store owners is that setting up so many Abandonment sequences will surely annoy their subscribers. If every interaction on the site triggers a sequence of emails following them up, surely this will be overkill?

Yes, it would. The main purpose of setting up these sequences isn't to bombard your subscribers with emails every time they interact with your site. Notice how in the Product and Category Abandonment stages in particular, a follow up sequence is not triggered at the last step? This is an important detail.

Not all of these sequences need to be necessarily attached to email follow ups. The Cart Abandonment is of course going to send follow up emails after it's triggered. But the others may execute without your subscribers ever even knowing. Instead, the Browse Abandonment sequences fire and run silently in the background, helping keep customer data up to date and informing the rest of your automation system what should be sent to this subscriber in the future.

Building the Semantic Automation

As we've covered, the Semantic Automation for eCommerce is composed of four automations: Category Abandonment, Product Abandonment, Cart Abandonment and Checkout Abandonment. Now we'll look at how to build each of these inside your EMS.

Just as with the implementation section from the Dispersal stage, the exact methods for how to build these sequences will vary greatly. It depends largely on which EMS you choose to use. For example, setting up the sequences in *ActiveCampaign* is different to doing so with *Mailchimp* or *Klaviyo*. While the individual steps themselves may be different, the underlying mechanics for how these sequences work are all the same.

Just as with the Dispersal stage, it's the strategy that's important, not the minor details. What I want to get across is a high-level understanding of the mechanics behind each of these sequences. By understanding what's happening and why, you'll be better informed to set these up for yourself, no matter which platform you ultimately go with. Let's look at how to actually build each one in more detail.

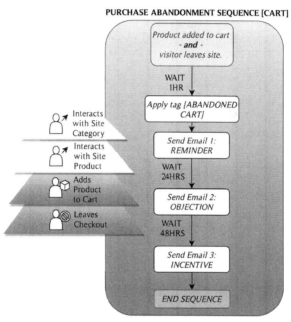

A Cart Abandonment sequence.

Cart Abandonment

As the value of these sequences becomes increasingly apparent, users have begun to expect this as a basic function and increasingly as a non-negotiable. EMS developers have responded in kind, and the most popular solutions now have these sequences built in. Even free solutions with relatively basic features such as *Mailchimp* now have native support for setting up Cart Abandonment, with integrations to match a wide variety of different eCommerce content management systems.

The result of this being a core feature is that it is usually trivially easy to set up, sometimes with guided templates and instructions for how to do so.

Triggers

So the first step is to either select the option equivalent to "Create abandoned cart sequence", or saving that, simply creating a new blank automation template where you'll build your own from scratch.

If you're building your own, the first thing you need to do is select the trigger that executes the automation. In the case of Cart Abandonment, this trigger will be the following conditions set as true in your EMS automation builder:

- *Product added to cart - **and** - visitor leaves site.*

In practice, you probably won't even need to define those variables yourself. You can just use the "out of the box" solution. Once you've set up Site Tracking, most EMS have a pre-built option for an abandoned cart start trigger. Selecting the "user abandoned cart" (or similar) starting trigger for your new automation is probably the best option if it's available.

Emails

Now you've set up site tracking and you've selected a starting trigger. The following is a template for how to design an effective Cart Abandonment email follow up sequence. Again, your EMS may already have a template they recommend you use and doing so is at your discretion. But in general, a typical sequence of this type follows the formula of "ROI" – Reminder, Objection, Incentive:

- **The Reminder email**'s purpose is, as the name implies, a simple reminder. You create an opportunity for the customer to close the loop on their purchase. You mention that something has been left behind in the cart, and that it is being held for purchase. Include a clear call to action that takes the subscriber back to their cart to complete the purchase.

- **The Objection email** comes next and is intended to handle a perceived barrier to the sale. This might take the form of a common complaint (expensive shipping costs? Unexpected taxes?), or perhaps unclear checkout user experience.

  The data gathered by Site Tracking and looking at the patterns of your user behavior will make this objection clearer over time. Whatever the case, bring up the objection in this email while again presenting a clear call to action to complete the purchase.

- **The Incentive email** is the final one, and this is where it can be effective to offer a discount or voucher code to persuade your shopper to complete their purchase.

  Sometimes marketers begin the Cart Abandonment sequence with an incentive, but it's unnecessary. Wait until you have first been reminded and then handle any remaining objections before offering a discount or free shipping. Many times, the initial simple reminder will be enough to get the customer to convert.

When implemented, an idealized Cart Abandonment sequence has steps that look something like this:

1. Trigger executes: Visitor abandoned cart.
2. Wait for one hour.
3. Apply Tag: ABANDONED CART
4. Send email: Reminder
5. Wait for 24 hours.
6. Send email: Objection
7. Wait for 48 hours.
8. Send email: Incentive

Checkout Abandonment

The next automation we'll build is Checkout Abandonment. As already mentioned, this is often confused with Cart Abandonment. However it's worth looking at what conditions actually comprise the triggers for your default "Abandonment" sequence inside your EMS. So while many

EMS provide "Cart Abandonment" out of the box, sometimes the conditions that trigger this sequence are actually the conditions that should be used to trigger an abandoned checkout.

The result is many store owners build what they think is a Cart Abandonment sequence but turns out to actually be Checkout Abandonment. I must stress that the gulf that exists between the two is vast. Setting up both of these is essential to improve conversion rates. Not only do you miss out on a full picture of the customer journey, but the number of visitors abandoning their carts is far higher than those abandoning at checkout stage. So by only setting up Checkout Abandonment, store owners are unknowingly missing out on a huge number of potential sales.

Triggers

In contrast to the starting conditions of Cart Abandonment, Checkout Abandonment begins with a trigger more like "user has visited page: (checkout url)". This is an important distinction because while the trigger for Cart Abandonment was an item being added to the cart, this doesn't matter so much for this sequence. They can't access the checkout unless they have an item already in their cart to begin with.

In any case, setting up Checkout Abandonment is relatively straightforward. The first step is to create a new blank automation template. With the automation builder open, the first thing you need to do is select a trigger that executes the automation. In the case of Checkout Abandonment, this trigger will be the following condition as true:

- *Product added to cart -* ***and*** *- user has visited the page: [Your Checkout URL].*

Emails

After setting up the new automation and the starting trigger, the next step is to design the steps of the automation itself. We'll just reuse the same emails we used in the Cart Abandonment sequence. The goal of the two sequences is the same - catching a lost sale and converting it. The distinction is that they catch the abandonment at different points of the customer journey.

So what we'll do is simply add a condition to make sure subscribers aren't being sent the same emails twice. We'll make it so if someone adds to cart and abandons, they'll get sent the Cart Abandonment sequence, but if they don't abandon there and instead make it all the way to Checkout Abandonment, it will trigger at that point.

So again, a typical Checkout Abandonment sequence follows the formula of "ROI", or, Reminder, Objection, Incentive. When implemented, an idealized Cart Abandonment sequence has steps that look something like this:

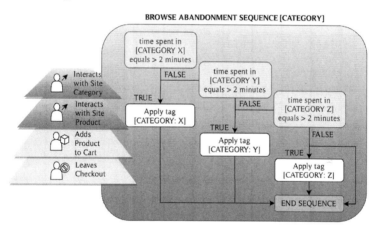

A Category Abandonment sequence.

1. Trigger executes: Product added to cart - and - user has visited the page: [Your Checkout URL].
2. Contact is not in automation: Cart Abandonment.
3. Begin Automation: Cart Abandonment.

Product and Category Abandonment

The final two automations are similar with regards to setup.

Again, some EMS will provide a "Browse Abandonment" feature similar to a default Cart Abandonment. This can sometimes cause confusion as the exact trigger is unknown - is it Product or Category Abandonment? It can be hard to tell. A lot of the time, this trigger is something like "Viewed product", and is rarely anything to do with the category level of the browsing stage of the buyer's journey. So the best way to be sure is to set this up manually.

Triggers

As with the other automations, the first place to start is creating a new blank automation. From there, you'll add your starting trigger.

For **Product Abandonment**, these triggers can be:

- *"Visited X product N times during session"*. This will then apply a tag in the EMS such as "PRODUCT: Shirt".

For **Category Abandonment**, these triggers can be:

- *"time spent in [category:shirts] equals > 2 minutes"*. We can use this trigger to then apply a tag, something like "CATEGORY: Shirts".

You might be wondering what emails you should send those subscribers who meet Category or Product-level abandonment triggers? Surely sending email follow ups to these subscribers will be a bit too much? I'd agree with that observation. Sending too many follow up emails from browsing activity, rather than improving conversions, can of course come across as creepy.

While we definitely want to use the data gathered from the browse abandonment sequences to inform our offers for that subscriber, we don't want to overtly send follow ups as with the Cart and Checkout

Abandonment sequences. Instead, these two sequences will be used to help build the Semantic Layer. Once data about browsing activity has been sent back to the EMS and the behaviors satisfy the above triggers, the sequence will simply apply a tag which progressively builds up a profile about that subscriber.

Let's look at how we use the data gathered from the browse abandonment sequences to build highly personalized emails that improve conversions.

Putting It All Together

Now that the sequences are set up, how do we actually capitalize on this data we're collecting? How do we personalize emails to improve conversions? Broadly, there are two main strategies for personalizing product-aware emails.

1. Product and Category Awareness Sequences

The most straightforward way to personalize the customer journey is by building multiple Product Aware sequences for individual categories or products.

For example, Let's say Subscriber X visits your site from an email you sent. While on the site, the subscriber explores the "Shirts" category, and spends significant time on a specific product, "White Shirt".

If you have the abandonment sequences set up correctly, the above behavior will be tracked and sent back to your EMS. After a while you may discover a large number of subscribers are being tagged "INTEREST: White Shirt". So you can then confidently create a dedicated Product Aware sequence of 3-5 emails for White Shirts.

When that tag is added to the subscriber, it also triggers the sequence. This personalizes the customer experience using the *Semantic Layer*. By using the tags from the Browse Abandonment sequences, we trigger these more targeted sequences which show more relevant and timely information, and thus have a higher likelihood of conversion.

Natural Orders

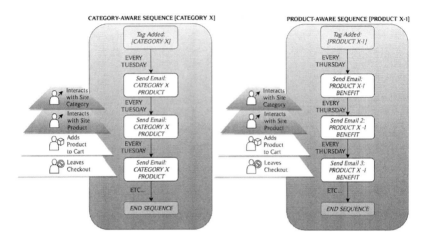

Product and Category Abandonment Sequences

A couple things to note about these sequences:

- The difference between Category and Product Abandonment is important. When a subscriber visits your site and reaches the point where they're given a Product tag, they will likely have also triggered a Category Abandonment sequence.

  What this means is that this subscriber will receive both the Category and Product sequences. These will both be based on expressed interests, so it's good personalization, but make sure these emails aren't being sent on the same day and are spaced apart. For example, you can see in the above Figure that category-level emails are scheduled to go out on Tuesdays, and product-level emails are scheduled for Thursdays.

- It's also important to make sure to end one sequence before you begin another. Set up additional tags to ensure that when a subscriber visits your site and has new browse abandonment tags for a different category or product, that this cancels or limits the amount of other sequences of this type that are currently active.

2. Campaign Segmentation

Another way the Semantic Automation is useful is for sending once-off campaigns. This is important for when you create sales, promotions or discounts. Instead of sending a discount on a specific product to your entire list, you can send it only to those subscribers who have expressed interest in that product or category.

The reason you may want to do this is because it will limit the amount of irrelevant offers you send to your list, while also maximizing the conversions you receive from each campaign you run. You'll save those who aren't interested from being exposed to "spam", but for those who actually are interested it will again appear like more value.

To do this, simply use the segmenting features inside your EMS to only send campaigns to users with a certain tag.

What's next? Now you've built a system for recruiting new subscribers into your email database environment, and you've enabled the ideal conditions for them to establish themselves as new customers.

Now that you've built the foundations for an environment where buying behavior flourishes, the next step is to enhance the conditions for further growth and enable those who have already purchased to do so again (and again).

In the next chapter, we're going to go into more detail about these types of once-off campaigns. We'll look at how nature again has lessons for us in how we can find extremely profitable customer segments in our list, and a series of strategies we can use to make every conversion as profitable as possible.

Summary

- **The goal of the Recruitment stage is to establish new paying customers by converting Product-Aware prospects.** While the Recruitment stage was about creating that pool of prospects, this stage ensures that the journey they take to purchase is smooth and uninhibited.

- **To improve our conversions we need to focus on personalization**: and personalizing is really just about improving the *relevance* and *timing* of a given email.

- **The only way to do that is by understanding our customer.** The Black Box and Kotler's *Customer Journey* and *Customer Avatar* guide us in knowing where to look to do so.

- **But to actually collect and organize this data we must build *the Semantic Layer*.** We can then use this to segment, personalize, trigger automations and improve conversions.

DOWNLOAD FREE RESOURCES

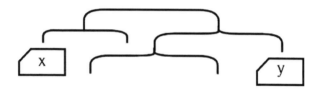

Remember, to access a free tag taxonomy planning document, as well as the other free resources that come with this book, please visit: symbiosgrowthautomation.com/natural-orders-resources

The Southern Cassowary (*Casuarius casuarius*). Credit: Torsten Pursche

III.
ESTABLISHMENT

When the Gondwana supercontinent began to break apart around fifty million years ago, much of the earth at that time was blanketed by thick rainforest. As the continents as we know them today slowly drifted apart from that single landmass, the world eventually plunged into a deep ice age, followed by a thawing that continues to this day.

The combination of drifting continental plates and increasing temperatures meant the ancient Gondwana rainforest of old all but disappeared. But some patches still remain. In the North-East of Australia, the Daintree Rainforest is one sizeable remnant: covering an area of 1200 square kilometers, it's the third largest rainforest in the world,[75] and at its higher altitudes, by far the oldest.

Dating back 180 million years, these sections of the Daintree are true prehistoric environments, with the species to match. There you'll find ancient trees such as the Antarctic Beech that once flourished in their namesake, the world's oldest known flowering plants,[76] the world's largest moth — the size of a bird with a thirty-centimeter wingspan[77] — and six-meter long saltwater crocodiles.

Taken together, it's easy to see why British naturalist Sir David Attenborough referred to the Daintree as *"the most extraordinary place on earth"*.[78] Representing just 0.12% of the Australian continent's landmass, this relatively small area contains around 50% of its total bird, butterfly, mammal and freshwater fish species.[79]

---

[75] Sightseeingtoursaustralia.com.au. Why is the Daintree Rainforest Important? [ONLINE] Available at: https://sightseeingtoursaustralia.com.au/tips-articles/why-is-the-daintree-rainforest-important/

[76] Australiangeographic.com.au. The Idiot Fruit Tree - Australian Geographic [ONLINE] Available at: https://www.australiangeographic.com.au/topics/science-environment/2017/07/the-idiot-fruit-tree/

[77] Wettropics.gov.au. Butterflyfacts [ONLINE] Available at: https://www.wettropics.gov.au/site/user-assets/docs/butterflyfacts.pdf

[78] Youtube.com. Sir David Attenborough Endorses Tropical North Queensland - YouTube [ONLINE] Available at: https://www.youtube.com/watch?v=_EdXkEImSps&list=PL2fcnDR1IIEtzlPhQ1q_NSPTlwC7E21lW&index=6

[79] Wet Tropics Management Authority. World Heritage Area - facts and figures | Wet Tropics Management Authority [ONLINE] Available at: https://www.wettropics.gov.au/world-heritage-area-facts-and-figures.html

This number and variety makes the Daintree one of the most diverse ecosystems on earth. And with this diversity comes benefits for the entire planet. With millions of plants drawing energy from the sun, plus ample water and high levels of nutrients packed into a concentrated area, every year the Daintree is responsible for the creation of massive amounts of organic carbon — the basic building blocks of life.

This organic carbon is often used as a "key metric" for measuring the relative importance of an ecosystem. A lot like management consultants, ecologists refer to the amount of organic carbon an ecosystem produces as its level of "productivity". The more organic carbon produced, the more productive it can be said to be.

Using this measure, rainforests are among the most "productive" ecosystems on earth, followed by coral reefs, estuaries and wetlands. What these ecosystems have in common is that they are all relatively small areas accounting for the majority of organic carbon produced across the globe.

This seems to be a common pattern. Looking at the total surface area of our planet, life as we know it depends upon just a handful of relatively small, but critical, areas. But zoom into any of these critical areas, and the pattern appears to repeat again. In the Daintree for example, much of the total productivity can be traced back to a single species of bird.

The Southern Cassowary (*Casuarius casuarius*), a giant and strikingly coloured ratite (of the same family as ostriches and emus), is one such species. Like much else in the Daintree, this bird is something of a dinosaur: known for its aggressiveness, the Southern Cassowary has attacked and even killed humans.[80] In fact, its reputation is such that when the Cassowary patrols its large territorial boundaries, handlers have been known to use riot shields for self-protection.[81]

---

[80] Diamond, J. M. (1997) Guns, germs and steel: The fates of human societies. London, England: Jonathan Cape.

[81] Dailytelegraph.com.au. Australian Reptile Park keepers step in with riot shields during attempt to mate cassowaries | Daily Telegraph [ONLINE] Available at: https://www.dailytelegraph.com.au/newslocal/central-coast/australian-reptile-park-keepers-step-in-with-riot-shields-during-attempt-to-mate-cassowaries/news-story/7ae804e2f417c6372b927ecaf67b495f

But aside from the danger it poses, the Cassowary helps hold the Daintree together. Traveling large distances each day, this bird is one of the most important seed dispersal mechanisms in the rainforest. Many of the seventy types of fruit it eats and deposits across the rainforest floor would be untouched by other animals, which often find them toxic. Lacking the cassowary dispersing these seeds, the productivity of the Daintree ecosystem would be significantly reduced. So much so that ecologists refer to the Southern Cassowary as a "keystone species" – a species deemed essential for the functioning of the ecosystem it inhabits.[82]

It seems far-fetched. But this is actually a pattern we see over and over again in nature. Regularly, total outputs seem to be always attributable to just a small fraction of the components.

- The output of one of the most productive ecosystems on earth would be greatly reduced without this single keystone species.
- A reduction in output of this ecosystem would have far reaching consequences for the rest of the planet.
- One single species of bird plays an outsized role in the productivity of the entire planet.

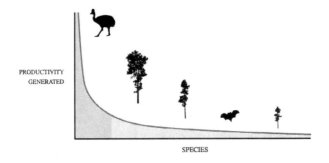

The Power-Law Distribution in nature

---

[82] Wet Tropics Management Authority. Cassowaries | Wet Tropics Management Authority [ONLINE] Available at: https://www.wettropics.gov.au/cassowaries

This pattern is sometimes referred to as a "power-law distribution". Looking at the graph above, the curve of the power law has a few defining features:

- A "tall head" on the left side, where a minority of total measurements produce the largest results.

- A "long tail" trailing out towards the right, where the majority of the measurements produce relatively minimal results.

It's staggering the way this one distribution describes so much in nature. You may not even realize how ubiquitous these distributions are. They occur everywhere around us, everyday:

- 80% of a tree's branches produce 20% of the leaves, and 20% of the branches produce 80% of the leaves.
- 80% of all known species on earth are insects (arthropods), and all other life makes up the other 20%.[83]
- Of these insects, 80% of all insects are beetles, 20% are all other insects.[84]
- 20% of those infected with a disease account for 80% of its spread.[85]
- 2% of the Earth's surface area is home to 50% of all plants and animals.[86]
- 20% of bird species make up 80% of sightings.[87]
- 1.4% of tree species account for 50% of total trees in the Amazon Rainforest.[88]

---

[83] Si.edu. Numbers of Insects (Species and Individuals) | Smithsonian Institution [ONLINE] Available at: https://www.si.edu/spotlight/buginfo/bugnos

[84] IISC (2011) "State of Observed Species," National Institute for Species Exploration. Available at: https://www.esf.edu/species/documents/sos2011.pdf.

[85] Cooper, L., Kang, S.Y., Bisanzio, D. et al. (2019) "Pareto rules for malaria super-spreaders and super-spreading," Nat Commun, 10(3939).

[86] Livescience.com. Facts About Rainforests | Live Science [ONLINE] Available at: https://www.livescience.com/63196-rainforest-facts.html

[87] Fred J. Rispoli and Suhua Zeng et al (2014) "Even birds follow Pareto's 80–20 rule," Significance (Oxford, England), 11(1), pp. 37–38.

[88] Livescience.com. A Few Tree Species Dominate Amazon Rain Forest | Live Science [ONLINE] Available at: https://www.livescience.com/40508-few-tree-species-dominate-amazon-rainforest.html

Once you're aware of the pattern, you'll start seeing it everywhere. And it's more than simple confirmation bias: these power laws really are something akin to a "Law of Nature", as far as we can say we have anything like that at all. At the very least, it's a very common pattern that in many guises underlies the way our world is organized.

Of course, these sorts of distributions aren't just limited to the natural world: they're also ubiquitous in business. What can we learn from this for our own Walled Garden ecosystem?

Establishment

The 80-20 distribution, or Pareto Principle, is a well-known example of a power law distribution regularly applied in business. It takes its name from the Italian economist Vilfredo Pareto, who first noticed a peculiar pattern in the distribution of wealth in Italy. Specifically, he noticed roughly 80% of total land ownership was attributable to around just 20% of the population.

Outside of Pareto's observation, some other more recent observations of the 80-20 principle have included:

- 20% of sales people are responsible for 80% of total sales revenue.
- 20% of customers account for 80% of total profits.
- 20% of the most reported software bugs cause 80% of software crashes.
- 80% of customers only use 20% of software features.
- 80% of your complaints come from 20% of your customers.
- 20% of a user's phone apps get 80% usage.

In fact, I'm willing to bet you can easily demonstrate the 80-20 principle in your own business. Try it for yourself. Open your Google Analytics dashboard. Set the date range to the past year. In the left-hand column go to Acquisition > Site Content > All Pages. In the main window, arrange your "unique users" column by descending order.

I'm confident you'll find that across all the pages of your site, a vast majority of your total traffic comes from just a handful of pages. While it may not be a perfect "80-20" ratio as consultant Perry Marshall describes in his book *80/20 Sales and Marketing*, I'm confident it will follow a power law distribution that is near to that ratio.

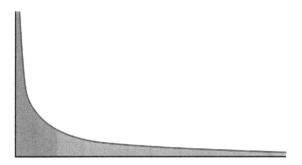

The Power-Law Distribution: The Minority of Instances Account for the Majority of Results

The Establishment stage is where we convert our ecosystem into a veritable Daintree: a productivity superpower; a thriving ecosystem.

If the cassowary were to be removed from the rainforest, the productive capacity of that system would be severely reduced. Similarly, without nurturing the equivalent of our own keystone species, we will never reach the potential of our own ecosystem of email marketing and automation.

In the Establishment stage, we seek to replicate this by improving the amount of revenue generated by our top customers. The overall revenue of the business will rise in turn. The success of certain "keystone" individuals in an ecosystem leads to the improved productivity of the overall system.

Archimedes is supposed to have said *"Give me a lever long enough and a fulcrum on which to place it and I shall move the world"*. Understanding the power laws in your business gives you that lever. The only unknown remaining is the fulcrum on which to place it.

STAGE	FOUNDATION	DISPERSAL	RECRUITMENT	ESTABLISHMENT
GOAL	TSC	Engagement	Conversion	Lifetime Value
METHOD	Improve Optin Placements	Provide Value Progress Awareness	Personalization	Increase New Orders Increase Repeat Orders Increase Average Order Value
AUTOMATIONS	N/A	Awareness Automation	Semantic Automation	LTV Automation

The Constraints to Growth

Justus von Liebig's *Law of the Minimum* states that *"Growth is dictated not by total resources available, but by the scarcest resource"*.[89]

Liebig was an influential 19th century German scientist, known primarily as one of the pioneers in the field of organic chemistry. But he was something of a savant, and made dozens of contributions to a variety of fields. Specifically, it was in his innovations in plant nutrition where he applied his now famous "Law of the Minimum".

Liebig knew what nutrients were essential requirements for a plant to grow. But he noted that the optimal growth of a plant was dependent upon having sufficient levels of *all* of these essential nutrients. While all could be *present*, it would be the one nutrient that was *lacking* in comparison to others that would always be the bottleneck to growth.

This is sometimes illustrated using a device known as "Liebig's Barrel".

Imagine a barrel of vertical wooden panels, but it's old and worn out: while most of the panels of the barrel are full-length, some of them are broken at different points, making some shorter than the others. The

---

[89] R.R. van der Ploeg, W. Böhm, M.B. Kirkham, (1999), On the origin of the theory of mineral nutrition of plants and the law of the minimum, Soil Science Society of America Journal 63, 1055–1062.

result is that when the barrel is filled with water, the maximum amount it can carry is limited by its shortest broken panel. The water will simply flow from this opening.

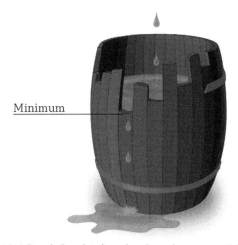

Liebig's Barrel: Growth is dictated not by total resources available, but by the scarcest resource.

Liebig's Law of the Minimum and by extension, his "Barrel", illustrate something similar to the saying *"a chain is no stronger than its weakest link"*. If a plant were growing in soil deficient in, say, nitrogen, then that limited nutrient would be the factor inhibiting optimal growth.

Liebig eventually tested this and applied it to the successful formulation of some of the first fertilizers containing ammonia (a nitrogen-rich compound). He continued refining this formulation to produce the basis of modern fertilizers, now one of the most widely manufactured products in industrial chemistry.

How does all this apply to your business? Just like the panels of Liebig's Barrel, his Law of the Minimum can be used as a tool to break down your marketing "system" into its individual components. It instructs us to identify which of the components of our system are the weakest.

It's only by addressing the weakest component in the system that the system can improve in totality.

So the growth of our business is limited by its weakest constraint. But how do you then actually apply this? The most difficult part of utilizing Liebig's Law of the Minimum is uncovering what the components of the system actually are in the first place.

Traffic, Conversion, Lifetime Value

In the book *80/20 Sales and Marketing,* Perry Marshall outlines the three components you can address to grow your business. Together, these three components make up the total potential output of your marketing efforts:

1. **Traffic**: If traffic is insufficient, there is no initial fuel.
2. **Conversion**: If conversions are poor, the traffic will be underutilized.
3. **Lifetime Value (LTV)**: If LTV isn't optimized, traffic and conversions aren't reaching their maximum potential.

Just like Liebig's Barrel, the weakest of these three components will be the place where the "leaks" occur. If any one of these three areas lag in your marketing strategy, you can be sure it will be inhibiting the overall growth of your business.

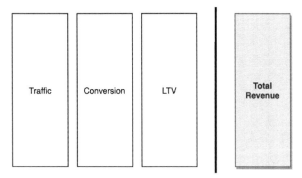

Traffic, Conversion and LTV are the three components of any marketing system.

So, having identified these three constraints, how do we know which one is limiting growth? If you're at the point in your business where you've built an email list, I'll assume you already have some Traffic coming to your site. Also, since we've just covered the Dispersal and Recruitment stages, let's also assume our Conversions are relatively well optimized.

The one component that we so far haven't addressed is LTV. So with the other two factors, our current constraints likely look something like this:

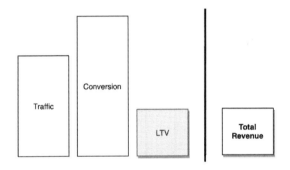

Assuming traffic is moderate, and the Dispersal and Recruitment stages have been implemented, the primary constraint will now be LTV.

Understanding Liebig's Law of the Minimum, the LTV constraint is the best place to focus our attention. It's the shortest plank in the broken barrel, the factor limiting the total output of the system.

Interestingly, this is exactly the opposite of what many small online business owners often do. More commonly, "more traffic" seems like the answer to all problems, when in fact there are more important, and often simpler, improvements that can be made instead.

This means that the main constraint to our system, the area which we must focus on according to the Law of the Minimum, is LTV. But what exactly is LTV? How can we measure it? And what is the point of improving LTV in the first place?

Lifetime Value [LTV]

Put simply, LTV estimates the value of your relationship with a customer. It estimates how much revenue a new customer will be worth to your business over their "lifetime", or the period of time in which they continue transacting with you.

First, let's look at how to calculate LTV. There are dozens of methods for this, some quite sophisticated. In order to illustrate its basic components, a simple formula for LTV could be:

(AVERAGE ORDER VALUE) X (PURCHASES PER YEAR) X AVERAGE CUSTOMER LIFETIME [YEARS])

Think back to Hayley's store selling plants. A frequent customer (Customer A) who regularly buys plants from Hayley might have an LTV something like this:

Customer A
(average order value = $100) x (purchases = 4 plants per year) x (buys for = 8 years)
In other terms: ($100) x (4) x (8) or **$3200**

Not bad for one customer. Now imagine a different customer (Customer B). Imagine this customer has an LTV like this:

Customer B
(average order value = $100) x (purchases = 2 plants per year) x (buys for = 3 years)
In other terms: ($100) x (2) x (3) or **$600**

That's a pretty big difference. Customer A is worth more than five times as much as Customer B, even though they're buying the same product at the same price. The main differences between these two customers are the length of relationship and the frequency of purchases, two important factors we'll get to later.

But more immediately, which of these customers should you be paying more attention to? Clearly, Customer A. From this example, the combined revenue of the two customers is equal to $3800. The revenue attributable to Customer A accounts for around 85% of the total. So it's clear from this example that there are huge gains to be made from improving the LTV constraint.

In fact, the most successful companies in the world owe their success to an in-depth understanding of their customer's LTV. The coffee franchise Starbucks, for example, knows that every new customer that walks in and buys a cup is worth thousands of dollars. They know that while there will be many customers who buy one cheap filter coffee and never return, there will be others who buy a $5 pumpkin spice latte every workday for the next ten years. There will be others still who also buy every new themed mug or logo-branded coffee machine, costing hundreds of dollars each.

The first customer who comes in to just buy the cheapest filter coffee probably only has an LTV of around $2. They bought a cheap product once and never returned to make another transaction. The other customer who buys coffee every day, in addition to every piece of Starbucks merch you can think of, may have an LTV of $20000 or higher.

With one customer having an LTV of $20000, and another customer only bringing in an LTV of $2, it becomes obvious who we should focus on to improve the overall revenue of our business. It's here that we see the power law distribution on full display.

Just as the Cassowary creates outsized results for its environment, your high LTV customers can be the source of massive gains in revenue that take your business to the next level.

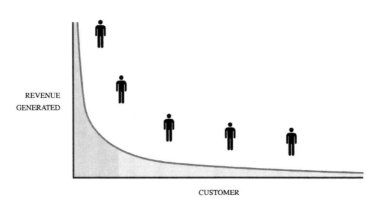

The Power Law Distribution: High LTV Customers

Improving LTV is what enables you to turn your email ecosystem into a Daintree Rainforest. Calculating LTV gives you valuable insights: who your best customers are; your most profitable products; and where value accrues in your business. You can then focus on continuing to deliver maximum value to your best customers and products: those 20% who yield 80% of revenue.

Without improving your LTV, you'll never truly realize the value of your database. By ignoring the power laws describing the ways value accrues in your business, you're leaving untapped revenue locked away in the hidden potential of your top customers.

Let's look at some other ways improving LTV can help take your business to the next level.

A properly tracked LTV will take your marketing strategy to the next level

LTV is the starting point to figuring out exactly how much you can profitably spend to acquire a new customer of the same type. This means you'll have a better idea of the ROI of different marketing strategies.

Instead of hoping for the best, you will instead be able to scenario-test the efficacy of different marketing directions before you fully commit to them. This opens up all sorts of new marketing channels that may have previously been prohibitively expensive: press, advertising or paid partnerships, for example.

High LTV equals high customer loyalty

LTV is a great measure of customer loyalty. The longer a customer sticks around, the more loyal they are — there isn't a clearer falsifiable metric for loyalty in business that I can think of.

Building on this, a high LTV can be a good indicator of high product quality. The first sale is a great milestone, but the sign of a truly well-loved brand are products that customers keep returning to purchase again and again. While many brands successfully lead a new subscriber through the labyrinth of Dispersal and Recruitment to attain the first sale, there are fewer who can then also attain a high LTV.

It also shifts your focus: you'll be continually devising ways to delight and add value to each experience your most loyal and profitable customers have with your brand.

Focusing on LTV is the best way to improve profitability

Most importantly, as the power laws demonstrate, LTV is the most powerful leverage we have for growing our business.

You can always find ways to send more traffic to your store and squeeze out incremental improvements in conversions. Both of these things are necessary — but they have their limits. The most *efficient* way to improve revenue is, by far, focusing on those customers right on your doorstep, already recruited inside your email database ecosystem.

It's more profitable to focus on your existing customers not only because they're more likely to spend more, but because it also saves you both time and money. In fact, it can be anywhere from 5 to 25x more expensive to find a new customer than it is to retain an existing one.[90]

This makes intuitive sense: instead of going out to search for some ethereal image of what you imagine your customer avatar to be, you can instead focus on the *actual* market right in front of you, which you also happen to already have a huge amount of data on. They're already there, they've already shown buying behavior, and they're the best example of your market you'll find anywhere — sell to them.

Understanding how important it is to improve LTV, how do we actually go about doing so? Just as we found the limit to growth across the components of Traffic, Conversion and LTV, we can also do the same again for LTV.

Turtles All the Way Down

In his 1917 book *On Growth and Form*,[91] Scottish mathematician D'Arcy Wentworth Thompson described the mathematics underlying dozens of natural phenomena: the formation of cells, the relationship between size and weight in animals, the rate of growth in trees, among many others.

On Growth and Form is today considered a classic. It's regularly prescribed as required reading in many undergraduate architecture courses and it has influenced the work of dozens of prominent figures, from computer scientist Alan Turing and anthropologist Claude Lévi-Strauss. It was instrumental in the development of the field of allometry: the study of the relationship of animal body size to shape, anatomy, physiology, and behavior.

In the book, Thompson details many of the fractals ubiquitous in the natural world. These can be seen in an endless number of examples

---

[90] Hbr.org. The Value of Keeping the Right Customers [ONLINE] Available at: https://hbr.org/2014/10/the-value-of-keeping-the-right-customers
[91] Thompson, D. W. (1942) On Growth and Form. Cambridge, England: Cambridge University Press.

— from the swirl of a snail's shell and the growth of branches of a tree; to the paths of lightning, rivers and the forms of mountains.

These phenomena all share the same underlying mathematical trait: the power law. In these examples, the power law distribution we described earlier not only exists, but it repeats within itself: infinite recursion. The repetition of a simple ratio at different scales results in the effect of an infinitely repeating pattern.[92]

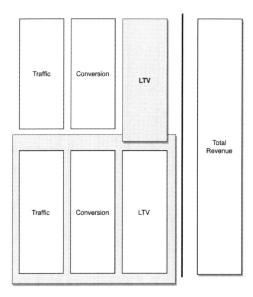

Recurring components in your marketing strategy.

Being based on power laws, our components of Traffic, Subscribers and LTV also demonstrate this infinitely repeating pattern. When you seek to improve one of the constraints inside the triangle - take Conversion, for example - you invariably come across yet another subset of the

---

[92] Komulainen, T. (no date) "Self-Similarity and Power Laws," Helsinki University of Technology Laboratory of Process Control and Automation. Available at: http://neocybernetics.com/report145/Chapter10.pdf.

components "Traffic, Conversion, LTV". Each individual component has another Traffic, Conversion and LTV component embedded inside it.

It's easier to understand with an example. Let's say you send a new campaign to your email list. In the email, there's a link to a landing page with a button to purchase a product.

- First, you must send the Traffic (your email list) to the page.
- On the page, factors influence the rate of Conversion (purchasing the product),
- LTV determines the value of that event (how much each purchase is worth).

So, while on one level you get a conversion rate for the whole campaign ("we converted x% of users"), when you zoom in, the pattern is there. There's another Traffic, Conversion, LTV power triangle occurring within each individual constraint.

Let's look only at this pattern inside the Conversion component:

- What percentage of the email list clicked to go to the page? (Traffic)
- What percentage of traffic to the page bought the product? (Conversion)
- What percentage of those who purchased did so again later? (LTV)

This is "open to click" conversion, "click to add to cart" conversion, "cart to checkout" conversion, "checkout to purchase" conversion, *ad infinitum*. It's turtles all the way down.

Knowing this, it follows that in order to improve our LTV constraint, we must look at the components that make it up and address whichever is the weakest. It's Liebig's Law of the Minimum in effect again. With this in mind, what exactly are these sub-components that make up the LTV constraint?

Once we know this, we can easily know what we need to focus on to improve LTV.

The Three Ways to Improve LTV

Marketing consultant Jay Abraham has said:

"There are only three ways to increase your business:

1. *Increase the number of clients, get more new prospects into paying customers.*

2. *Increase the size of the average transaction, get each client to buy more at each purchase.*

3. *Increase the frequency that the average client buys from you, get each customer to buy from you more often."*

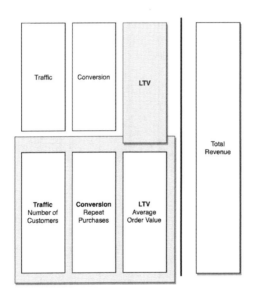

The LTV factor contains sub-components which limit its overall output.

Abraham's formulation just happens to perfectly describe the three types of constraints inside LTV.

There are only three ways to grow your business: get more customers (that's increasing traffic to the LTV constraint), increase repeat purchases (more conversion), or increase the amount spent at each transaction (LTV, again).

So we know exactly where we need to focus in order to improve our LTV. Let's look at how this might work in an example.

Let's say that on average you get 200 customers per month. The average transaction is $50 and customers only purchase once. This means you bring in $10,000 per month.

Customers	Average Transaction	Purchase Frequency	Revenue
200	$50	1	$10,000

Your conversions stay the same and average transaction and purchase frequency don't move. You go about growing your business in a way common to many store owners — you work very hard at your traffic strategy. After a month appealing to the whims of the almighty algorithm on your social media platform of choice, you manage to bring in an additional 30 customers the next month:

Customers	Average Transaction	Purchase Frequency	Revenue
230	$50	1	$11,500

This results in a 15% increase in revenue. While it's definitely worth celebrating an extra $1500, let's for a moment consider the alternative to toiling over a temporary traffic spike for a single month.

Imagine instead you implement a couple of simple changes that improve your average transaction and purchase frequency by smaller amounts.

Customers	Average Transaction	Purchase Frequency	Revenue
200	$55	1.1	$12,100

With just a tiny 10% increase in both average transaction and purchase frequency, you end up with an additional $2100 - a 20% increase in revenue — *without adding a single additional customer.*

This is where the benefits of email marketing automation really become apparent. The best part about these small cumulative gains is that they can be 100% automated and delivered to your customers while you sleep. Just like the Starbucks customers who will buy every product available, your business has high value, power law customers who *want* to spend more. You can dramatically increase your revenue just by leveraging the power laws that already exist in your business.

You have the lever, and you can now reliably identify the best fulcrum on which to place it. For this reason, the Establishment stage is arguably the most valuable, if not the most important of the Stages of Succession in the *Natural Orders* system. While you need the foundation built in the *Dispersal* stage, and you need to optimize initial conversions in *Recruitment*, the best way to use email marketing and automation to dramatically grow your business is through unlocking LTV as we've demonstrated here.

Lifetime Value Automation

We now have the three factors we know will remove the LTV constraint to our revenue by improving LTV:

1. Increasing the average transaction value.
2. Increasing the frequency of repeat purchases from existing customers.
3. Increasing the number of new customers.

In practice there are an almost endless number of ways you can address each of these. Improving LTV is the infinite game of marketing, with each new project you take on bringing unique challenges, with unique solutions. Reading case studies of the ways talented marketers have grown businesses is one way to come across creative and novel solutions you hadn't thought of.

For that reason, this section and the Establishment stage in general will be somewhat less prescriptive and systematized than the Dispersal and Recruitment stages. While the previous stages had implementation plans to apply to your own business, this stage necessitates a bit more thought into how you will apply the following strategies.

That being said, combining the following automation strategies with the frameworks we've covered already will arm you with the tools and knowledge necessary to make the right decisions. You'll be able to look at the power laws inherent to your business, understand the constraints inhibiting your growth, and go about addressing those constraints in a way that makes growth as efficient as possible. Combining this with the foundations built in the previous two chapters will be the best possible primer for how to use email marketing automation profitably and sustainably.

Let's look at some of the strategies for addressing each individual LTV component.

1. Increase Average Order Value

The first way to improve our LTV is by addressing the constraint of Average Order Value (AOV). Increasing AOV means increasing the amount of value exchanged at each purchase. This usually means either purchasing higher quantities of a single product or buying other products in addition to the main purchase.

AOV can broadly be improved by three strategies:

1. *Upsells*: AOV is increased by upgrading to a more expensive version.
2. *Cross-Sells*: AOV is increased by selling complementary products at purchase.
3. *Bundling*: complementary products are promoted together at a reduced overall price to the customer but with maintained profitable margins and higher AOV for the seller.

Let's explore each type in more detail:

Upsells

We've all experienced an upsell at some point: upgrading a hotel room to a superior one, buying a new car model with add-on features, or being convinced to convert a long-haul flight ticket from economy to business.

Upsells increase AOV by offering a more expensive version of the product being purchased. The upsell builds upon the value of the base product — it solves the same problem, but in a slightly more compelling way, thus commanding a higher price. This means it should be perceived by the customer as superior to the base model: it adds additional features, guarantees or other factors which build on the benefits offered by the original product.

The wisdom of upsells lies, again, in the exploitation of the power law distribution inside your customer database. Let's say each month you sell 100 units of Product X at $100 each, yielding $10,000 revenue with an AOV of $1000.

Customers	Average Transaction	Average Purchase Frequency	Revenue
100	$100	1	$10,000

You introduce a superior version of Product X, priced at $225, offered at the checkout as an upgrade for your customers. Given a conservative industry-wide average of 4% upsell conversion[93], this results in a 5% increase in revenue to $10,500, and a 5% increase in AOV to $105.

Customers	Average Transaction	Average Purchase Frequency	Revenue
100	$105	1	$10,500

---

[93] Crazyegg.com. How to Profit from Upsells, Cross-Sells and Bundles [ONLINE] Available at: https://www.crazyegg.com/blog/upsells-cross-sells-bundle-sells/

Compounded, this one small addition to this store will yield an additional $6000 revenue each year, a 5% increase. All from introducing one simple upsell product to your power law customers. These are customers who are already willing to hand over that money: the top 20% of your customers who *want* the option of purchasing a superior product. It takes very little extra work for significant gain - an easy win.

Broadly, the easiest way to build your first upsell offer is by using an existing third party plugin. Here are some common eCommerce solutions and some plugins that work well for each:

- *Shopify*: Product Upsell by Bold Commerce, One Click Upsell by Zipify.
- *WooCommerce*: One Click Upsells by WooCurve.
- *Magento*: Unlimited Upsell
- *BigCommerce*: Unlimited Upsell, Boost Sales.

A few more things to consider when designing your own upsell for your unique product line:

- For certain products, such as consumables, an upsell can simply be greater quantities of the same product at a bulk discount.

- Consider guarantees: Apple Computer's "AppleCare" insurance product offered with new computers is a highly profitable upsell tactic that improves their AOV significantly.

- Don't select upsells until a customer has selected a product. The tactic only works as a suggestion of additional value built on the problem being solved by the initial product.

- Don't add too many choices. Too many upsell options are more likely to result in no upsell at all. Make the decision simple and the additional value of the upsell clear.

- Don't be aggressive. The point of an upsell isn't to "extract more value" from each customer - it's to provide maximum value to those customers who are happy to pay for top-shelf versions of your products.

- Test and Track. Make sure you're tracking the effectiveness of the upsell. If it's not converting around or above the average 4%, try reconfiguring your offer so that it more clearly demonstrates value to your customers. You probably won't get it perfect the first time, but once it's set up it will continue to add value on its own.

- As with all "industry averages", don't let this limit your expectations. As we saw with the industry standard for open rates and traffic to subscriber conversion, these are, simply put, quite poor. Imagine the impact of your revenue if your upsell instead converts at 10% or 15%?

Cross-Sells

Cross-sells are often conflated with upsells, but there's an important difference. While upsells offer a superior version of a product for a higher price, a cross-sell aims to sell an additional product in conjunction with the primary purchase.

An upsell is more like an upgrade, whereas a cross-sell is more like "Do you want fries with that?". In fact, that's one of the classic examples of this tactic. The products offered in a successful cross-sell adds to the experience or utility of the main product being purchased. Anything that you can add on to complement the main purchase is a good candidate for a cross-sell. Earbuds to go with your new phone, web hosting for your new domain purchase, or oat milk for your latte.

So why bother implementing cross-sells in your store? Let's look again at our example, starting with the same conditions:

Customers	AOV	Average Purchase Frequency	Revenue
100	$100	1	$10,000

Now add a cross-sell opportunity at checkout, a complementary product priced at $25. Given a 35% conversion (the same conversion boasted by Amazon)[94], this results in a ~9% increase of AOV to $108.75, and a corresponding ~9% increase in revenue to $10,875.

Customers	AOV	Average Purchase Frequency	Revenue
100	$108.75	1	$10,875

Looking at the compounded result, this small addition will yield an extra $10,500 revenue over a year, an increase again of ~9%. All from introducing one simple cross-sell product. Again, very little extra work for a decent gain. You get a decent revenue bump and take advantage of yet another opportunity to provide extra value and appear helpful to your customers.

Building cross-sells can be achieved using most of the same plugins covered for upsells. But there are some things to consider when thinking about how to structure cross-sell offers:

- Be careful not to make your cross-sell items too expensive. A successful cross-sell shouldn't increase the base order value for more than around 25%. So, if selling a $100 item, don't offer cross-sell opportunities that cost more than $25.

- Offer cross-sells you know your customers might forget, but will want or require: filters for lenses, strings and picks for guitars, or batteries and refills, for example.

- Accessories also make great cross-sell items: examples include cases, covers, tripods or cleaning kits.

- Cross-sells can also be related or recommended products in that category. Amazon does this with great success in their "Customer who bought this also bought" section.

---

[94] The-future-of-commerce.com. E-commerce cross-sell and up-sell: The difference, benefits, and examples [ONLINE] Available at: https://www.the-future-of-commerce.com/2013/10/14/ecommerce-cross-sell-up-sell/

Bundling

Another strategy that combines the benefits of both cross-selling and upselling is Bundling. Bundling incorporates the best features of both: you offer complementary products as in cross-selling, while also convincing the customer to purchase a higher-margin product, as with upselling. The result, as with the others, is improved overall AOV. There are a number of benefits to using a bundling strategy as opposed to simply using cross-sells or upsells on their own.

Firstly, it makes shopping more convenient by reducing choices and providing a customer with everything they need to get maximum value from the product (accessories, add-ons, etc.) and make the transaction more frictionless. For example, if a customer buys a camera they'll also need to buy specific lenses, batteries, memory cards, cases and straps to get the most out of the product.

Secondly, a bundled offer for a customer seeking to use the camera in a specific way can be a great way to target a customer segment while also taking advantage of cross-sells and upsells. For example, a package targeting "beginner" photographers will save the customer time from having to research or otherwise figure out what they'll actually need to use the product effectively, providing a valuable service alongside the product itself.

Not only is it a better experience for the customer, it enhances the perceived value of the offer. Using the camera example, bundling these products together allows the store owner to offer a reduced total price while still retaining profitable margins.

There are two main types of bundles you can use - pure and mixed. Broadly, a Pure bundle is when you create a *new* product that consists of items that *cannot be bought* individually. Mixed bundles combine several existing individual products into a discounted deal. As a general rule, some studies have found mixed bundles tend to perform slightly better than pure bundles, but both have the same effect of improving AOV.[95]

---

[95] Mckinsey.com. How retailers can keep up with consumers | McKinsey [ONLINE] Available at: https://www.mckinsey.com/industries/retail/our-insights/how-retailers-can-keep-up-with-consumers

Consider a camera store making 60 sales per month, split between three different products. Monthly revenue is $20,000, with an AOV of $333 due to the volume of orders being split between lower and higher priced products.

Unbundled	Camera	Lens	Memory Card	Revenue	AOV
Price	$500	$450	$75	$20,750	$345
Orders	25	15	20		

Now let's assume the store owner identifies a customer segment who is interested in purchasing this particular lens with this camera. The store owner bundles these items and offers them at a slight discount. The price of the bundle shows the customer the other items they may have forgotten they needed, and throwing in a free memory card will "sweeten the deal".

Instead of selling 25 cameras and hoping this customer segment buys the other components you know they want, by putting together a unique offer combining these products you actually both end up better off.

Bundled	Camera Bundle	Revenue	AOV
Price	$900 (~10% discount)		
Orders	25	$22,500	$900

This means conversions for this bundle are more likely, with the result of a higher AOV for this customer segment. That in turn means the store owner has now improved the LTV for this particular segment. This potentially opens up new marketing opportunities such as paid traffic for this offer, personalizes the customer experience (and subsequent conversions) by creating a tailored offer, stands out against potential competition for a profitable customer segment, while adding more revenue while you're at it.

Part of the reason bundling is effective is due to an effect known as *price anchoring*. For the customer who knows they want both the specific lens and the camera itself, they're more likely to select the bundle you're offering rather than shopping around. When they compare your bundle, with a cheaper price and additional products with what these items would cost separately, it makes conversion more likely as the added value is clearer.

Here are a few more things to consider when designing your own bundles:

- Bundling can be a great way to encourage your customers to try out new product lines: by using price anchoring and "sweetening the deal" with a new product line, you help create new buying behaviors and can introduce new product categories.

- Make sure you list the value of each item individually in the bundle to demonstrate the potential savings if the customer purchases. Make it known that this is the more affordable option by contrasting it to the prices of the individual components.

- Another way you can implement bundling is by offering free or reduced shipping. For a simple example, if your store ships flat-rate you can build this value into your margins and subsidize it for customers with high AOV. By specifying a minimum order value, you encourage customers to increase the amount they purchase in order to qualify for free shipping costs.

- Look closely at your store analytics to understand which products are being purchased most frequently, together, or sequentially. The patterns in this information will help you uncover potential areas for bundles that convert.

- You can use the same techniques in upselling and cross-selling to promote your bundles. When a customer adds a specific product to their cart, you can offer a one-click upgrade at checkout to "upsell" to the bundle.

2. Increase Repeat Purchases

Increasing repeat purchases means your customers come back to buy more than once. The effect of Repeat Purchases is far more dramatic than increasing AOV alone.

Consider again our example:

Customers	AOV	Average Purchase Frequency	Revenue
100	$100	1	$10,000

If you maximize your AOV by 10%, that's great, as we just saw. But if you can then increase the amount of times that an order takes place, your LTV dramatically and quickly compounds. And it's the compounding effect of repeat purchases *plus* increased AOV where we create the most gains in LTV and revenue:

Customers	AOV	Average Purchase Frequency	Revenue
100	$110	2	$22,000

Repeat purchases aren't just lucrative, they're also highly effective. It's significantly easier to sell to existing customers than it is to convert new ones. In fact, after the first purchase, there's a 32% chance a new customer will transact with your brand again within a year. Compare this to an industry-wide average *new* customer conversion rate of just 3%.[96]

Not only are they more than ten times more likely to buy than a new customer, this actually improves with each successive purchase. The 2020 Adobe Digital Economy Index reported that a customer who has purchased from your store *twice* before is then 9 times more likely to convert again than a new customer.[97]

It doesn't end there: not only are existing customers more likely to buy again, they're likely to spend more each time they transact. A Bain & Company report titled *The Value of Online Customer Loyalty* states that

---

[96] Smartinsights.com. E-commerce conversion rates benchmarks 2022 - How do yours compare? [ONLINE] Available at: https://www.smartinsights.com/ecommerce/ecommerce-analytics/ecommerce-conversion-rates/
[97] Business.adobe.com. Adobe Digital Economy Index | Adobe Analytics [ONLINE] Available at: https://business.adobe.com/ca/resources/digital-economy-index.html

after being loyal to a brand for over 30 months, a customer is likely to increase their AOV by around 67%.[98]

The combination of increased AOV with likelihood of repurchase reveals just how valuable existing customers are for your business. Some studies have even revealed these repeat purchases account for more than 40% of total eCommerce revenue, with a mere 5% lift in the number of customers who buy again accounting for between 25% to 90% increase in gross profit.[99]

In fact, the Adobe Digital Economy Index even reports that in many cases, up to 41% of the revenue of an eCommerce store is attributable to just 8% of its customers. What this demonstrates yet again is the prevalence and importance of the power law distribution in your business:

- Those who have purchased once represent the most valuable portion of your email list.
- Those who purchase a second time reveal themselves as an even more valuable portion, and so on. Turtles all the way down.

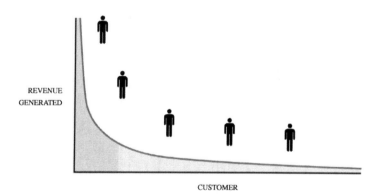

---

[98] Media.bain.com. The Value of Online Customer Loyalty and How You Can Capture It [ONLINE] Available at: https://media.bain.com/Images/Value_online_customer_loyalty_you_capture.pdf

[99] Hbr.org. The Value of Keeping the Right Customers [ONLINE] Available at: https://hbr.org/2014/10/the-value-of-keeping-the-right-customers

So how exactly do we capitalize on the compounding effects of repeat purchases? As with increasing AOV there are, in theory, countless ways to go about this, only limited by imagination. However, in an email and automation context there are a few best practice strategies we can use to capitalize on those customers who have already purchased.

- **Promotions and Discounts**: We can incentivise increased spend and additional purchases by encouraging brand loyalty through ongoing promotions and discounts.

- **Newsletters**: We'll also touch on the importance of newsletters as a strong contemporary trend in email marketing strategy that can encourage repeat purchases.

- **Loyalty and Advocacy**: We can broadly encourage repeat purchases with loyalty and advocacy strategies which couple exposing new products to existing customers with incentives to repurchase.

Let's cover each of these in a bit more detail:

Promotions and Discounts

So it should be clear we need to focus more attention on those subscribers who become customers, but how do we do this? How do we encourage repeat purchases for those who have bought from us once already?

The most straightforward way is by leveraging the data we've collected to target specific segments with opportunities to buy again. In the Recruitment stage, we ended by mentioning these once-off campaigns as a great way to implement personalization and increase conversions. These can improve first-time conversions for new customers, in line with the goals of that chapter, but they are also effective for improving repeat conversions for existing customers.

By using the data we collected in *the Semantic Layer*, it's possible to create highly targeted segments of subscribers with discrete interests. For example, you can create a subscriber search that includes only those who have viewed a certain product or product category, or only those who have engaged with emails within a certain time period. You can target individuals who have opened specific emails, clicked on specific links, or anyone who has abandoned a cart within a specified date range.

You can couple this level of segmentation with timely excuses for discounts and promotions. There are dozens of opportunities to send promotions and discounts throughout the year, some of them specifically suited to exciting certain niches or industries. For example, for one client selling luxury vegan leather products, events such as World Vegan Day are reliable and lucrative calendar dates for the brand. Planning for these types of events, in conjunction with smart segmentation, should be a priority.

Ongoing Newsletters

It's difficult to find a better example of the disruption we covered in the Walled Gardens chapter than tech company Substack. Launched in 2017, Substack is a platform that in their words *"make(s) it simple to start a publication that makes money from subscriptions"*. The authors writing on the platform build an audience on their own, attracting paying subscribers interested in niche topics the authors serve.

Substack is a perfect example of combining a supply and distribution advantage to disrupt an existing industry. In their own words, Substack writes on their site *"The internet has saturated us with an information deluge that has changed the economics of news. No one wants to add more noise to their lives, let alone pay for the privilege. But that is the very reason that the right kind of subscription content can be even more valuable in the digital age … Precisely targeted and curated content means less noise"*.[100]

The success of their platform proves their thesis. What the popularity of Substack and similar services proves is people are happy to pay a premium for relevant and niche content. As of writing, Substack now attracts over twelve million visitors per month, with over five hundred

---

[100] Chris Best. A better future for news [ONLINE] Available at: https://on.substack.com/p/a-better-future-for-news

thousand active paying subscribers. The audience is massive, and revenue similarly so, with the top ten most popular authors collectively grossing fifteen million dollars annually in subscription fees.[101] This is *the Curation Advantage* on full display.

What this means for your business is there's a huge opportunity to invest time into sending a newsletter that provides similar curated value. In a 2019 Forbes article titled *"Every Company is Now a Media Company"*, the author touches on this opportunity, stating that *"To stand out in today's media landscape, companies need to … start investing in high-quality media that uses audience insights and brand advocates to inform, entertain and inspire customer loyalty."* [102]

The benefits of providing timely, relevant value to your subscribers on an ongoing basis isn't just limited to keeping your brand top of mind or encouraging repeat purchases. It also allows you to grow your subscriber base as new subscribers join your list for the value of your newsletter. You solidify your brand positioning, maintain perception as an authority, and build a brand-matched audience to whom you can then effectively promote products and services.

Not only this, if you really invest time and effort into a newsletter, you can even build a subscription revenue stream of your own, just like the creators on Substack; one that complements your brand and creates traffic flow that's profitable in itself. Coupling this with other opportunities in this model such as paid endorsements can add significant revenue to your business outside of your core product line.

Loyalty and Advocacy

Another way to improve repeat purchases is by rewarding new customers. Loyalty, rewards, subscriptions or VIP programs are a common and effective way for stores to encourage those who purchase once to come

---

[101] Backlinko.com. Substack User and Revenue Statistics (2022) [ONLINE] Available at: https://backlinko.com/substack-users

[102] Nathan Pettijohn. Why Every Company Is A Media Company [ONLINE] Available at: https://www.forbes.com/sites/nathanpettijohn/2019/02/07/why-every-company-is-a-media-company/?sh=269d283b7391

back and do so again. While first time customers are already likely to come back and repurchase, by offering loyalty programs you increase the chances of this happening for both new and existing customers by enhancing incentives to do so.

The immediately obvious benefit is that these loyalty programs build revenue and LTV via repeat purchases. But revenue and LTV aren't the only benefits to these programs. A well-designed loyalty program can potentially attract brand new customers who aim to benefit from rewards other brands don't offer, potentially yielding a competitive advantage in your brand's positioning.

For example, some loyalty programs encourage their users to refer new customers in exchange for discounts. Doing so can turn your existing customers into brand advocates.[103]

A "VIP" program is another effective strategy which uses a clear hierarchy of membership tiers to project an ideal of exclusivity among top customers. Frequent flyer programs or "platinum-level" credit card products are one example of this, dividing participants into classes based on their activity within the program. When branded effectively, VIP programs can be a source of pride for certain customers who will increase repeat purchases just to maintain their place within a top tier of membership.

More general points programs also encourage repeat purchases. Many supermarket chains offer programs that encourage customers to do the majority of their shopping at their chain. In return these typically offer discounts, exclusives, free samples, coupons, or unreleased products to maintain a high LTV and mitigate the potential of lost customers to competitors.[104]

The revenue spent on attractive rewards for loyal customers is more than offset by the compounding effect of repeat purchases (and AOV) on LTV. In fact, certain types of loyalty programs can sometimes be

---

[103] Shopify.com. Ecommerce Loyalty Programs: 25 Strategies from 100+ Results & Stats [ONLINE] Available at: https://www.shopify.com/enterprise/ecommerce-loyalty-programs#1

[104] Rubygarage.org. Everything You Should Know About Ecommerce Loyalty Programs [ONLINE] Available at: https://rubygarage.org/blog/guide-to-online-loyalty-programs

profitable on their own. For example, Amazon's Prime membership subscription requires customers to pay a yearly fee, which in turn is used to make their rewards even more competitive: free same-day delivery and consistent generous discounts compound to make their platform more desirable for both new and existing customers.[105]

3. Increase New Customers

To recap: So far, we've determined the biggest constraint to our growth was LTV. The best way to improve this is by improving the sub-constraints of average order value and repeat purchases.

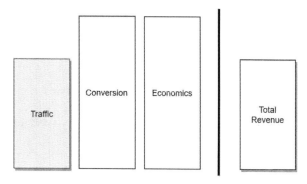

Traffic is now the limiting factor in the system.

Together, these two factors yield the greatest gains in LTV, helping us in our goal towards leveraging the largest possible gains from those individuals who contribute outsized revenue. We've taken advantage of the power laws underlying the structure of our email ecosystem.

With LTV addressed, it's now time to reapply the *Law of the Minimum* to uncover where we should focus our attention next. We look back to the constraints of Traffic, Conversion and LTV.

---

[105] Bigcommerce.com. Ecommerce Loyalty Programs: Reward Customers + Drive Sales (2021) [ONLINE] Available at: https://www.bigcommerce.com/blog/online-customer-loyalty-programs/#types-of-customer-loyalty-programs

Having addressed Conversions in Recruitment and LTV, at this point our total revenue is now only limited by one remaining factor. We're finally in a position where it makes sense to begin focusing on improving the *amount of traffic* arriving into our system.

New Channel Opportunities

When we used the example of Hayley earlier in the book, she was stuck in a cycle of dependency with her Instagram account. She needed to invest time and energy trying to figure out how to best game the algorithm, creating content and posts that were ultimately mostly for the benefit of that platform's users. She was working a vassal on borrowed land; her business was a *sink* that could never be self-sustaining.

But had she gone through the Stages of Succession with her email marketing ecosystem, Dispersal, Recruitment and now Establishment, Hayley's scenario couldn't be more different. Instead of relying entirely on the users she can attract from other Walled Gardens, Hayley would have built a garden of her own. In Voltaire's terms, she'd have truly *"cultivat(ed) (her) own garden"*.

With this, Hayley's opportunities for improving her traffic would now be better than ever. This is because improving LTV allows her to understand how much an average customer is worth.

With this information, we can now access new channels to acquire traffic. We now understand what a subscriber costs to acquire, so we can access new traffic channels beyond the scope of those originally available to us.

For example, if we know an average customer has an AOV of $106.25 and an Average Purchase Frequency of 2x per year, we know that we can spend anything up to $212.49 to acquire that customer, and still be profitable.

AOV	Average Purchase Frequency	Lifetime Value
$106.25	2	**$212.50**

Options such as Advertising, PR, and paid promotions and partnerships begin to make good business sense. These aren't just "risky bets", either: you now know what you can afford to pay for these new channels because you have a better understanding of your unit economics. And when you do send this traffic into your email marketing ecosystem, you'll know it's primed to make the most of it.

From Sink to Source, From Rocks to Rainforest

With all this in mind, we've come a long way since the first chapters. Starting with the *Dispersal stage*, we created the foundations for a favorable environment to attract new subscribers. By setting up the *Awareness Automation*, we built strong engagement while nurturing new arrivals so they'd be more likely to eventually purchase.

Next, we focused on getting those subscribers to convert. In the *Recruitment stage* we built a system that automatically monitors and labels the actions of our subscribers. In doing so, we gathered the data necessary to send out personalized emails, continuing to provide a valuable experience with a view to encourage purchases.

In this chapter, we've doubled down on our existing customers. By focusing on our most valuable subscribers, we've successfully *Established* our ecosystem. By understanding the power laws inherent to the structure of your email database, we've maximized its output and unlocked its true potential.

Coupling this with a tool to assess the current constraints in your business, you'll always have a way to look back to what your current limits are, and where to focus next in order to continue optimizing growth.

Summary

- **A power law distribution** describes many of the outsized effects found in nature. It also applies to business, known sometimes as the 80/20 rule or Pareto distribution. By focusing on this distribution in our email list we can focus on our top customer to improve LTV and increase revenue.
- **Using an analysis tool known as Liebig's Barrel** we can break down our marketing system into its constituent components and determine which area is the bottleneck. In a marketing context this is always going to be either Traffic, Conversion or LTV.
- **Focusing on your top customers is the best way to improve LTV.** Just like the Cassowary in the rainforest, there are some individuals who create outsized productivity, or in our case revenue, for the system they inhabit.
- Using Liebig's Barrel again, we can find that **the constraints for improving LTV are to either increase the number of new customers, the number of repeat purchases, or the average order value** These are sub-components of, and correspond respectively to, our Traffic, Conversion and LTV.
- **Average Order Value (AOV)** is best improved through upsells, cross-sells and bundling. **Repeat Purchases** are best improved via promotions, discounts, newsletters and loyalty or advocacy programs. **New Customers** are best improved by increasing traffic by leveraging your improved LTV to access paid channels.

CONCLUSION

Technique denies mystery a priori.
The mysterious is merely that which has not yet been technicized.

Jacques Ellul

Waldsterben roughly translates to "forest death". But unlike most German-English loan words, this one is relatively recent. First appearing around the middle of the 20th century, it saw wide usage around the same time as the collapse of the massive, state-planned forest plantations across Europe, and later, North America.

Many of these collapsing European forests, first planted in the mid-18th century, were the result of the first applications of "scientific forestry" practices. Around that time, Prussian and Saxon forest managers were devising methods to more precisely catalog the amount of harvestable timber in their forests.

This may sound mundane to a contemporary, with our increasing emphasis on data and measurement. But in the 18th century these techniques were cutting-edge. Today, most of us operate on the premise that everything we know can ultimately be broken down into components and "measured". But joined with this lay a hidden assumption: that *the only things which are real*, are those things *which we can measure*.

The cult 1999 book *Seeing Like a State* addresses this hidden assumption. According to author James C. Scott there's a type of blindness that can occur when we become over-zealous in our focus on data and measurement. Taken to the extreme, Scott explains how this particular type of blindness has resulted in many of the major planning and management catastrophes of the 20th century.

The *waldsterben* is an illustrative example. As the *technique* of the proto-German forest managers advanced, this led to massive tables of data, grouped into harvestable tree species, with growth, yield and revenue projections. It was maybe the first ever example of "big data".

Their efforts paid off, with timber output increasing in both volume and reliability. From there, these data-minded managers sought to further improve the efficiency of these forest "systems" they managed.

As they continually optimized toward a single metric of "*increased output of timber*", the data "blindness" began to take hold. They could now only see the forest in terms of how they were measuring it. According to Scott, *"the underbrush was cleared, the number of species was reduced (often to monoculture), and plantings were done simultaneously and in straight rows on large tracts"*.[106]

The resulting aesthetic became representative of the type of blindness that *Seeing Like a State* makes lucid: long running avenues of trees, uniform in size and species, easily accessible, measurable, and completely without surprise or complexity. Again via Scott, it was at this point that they *"… transform(ed) the real, diverse, and chaotic old- growth forest into a new, more uniform forest that closely resembled the administrative grid of its techniques"*.

The "legible" forest plantation. Credit: Willem van Aken, CSIRO

Scott describes the driving force behind this aesthetic as the seeking out of *"legibility"*: the physical manifestation of this problem of data blindness. For the forest managers, a neatly organized row of trees is *legible*, as opposed to a comparatively complex — and therefore *illegible* forest — growing unperturbed.

For a while, these new, highly *legible* forests were a success. They did again increase timber yields in the short term. The mechanical structure

---

[106] Scott, J. C. (1999) Seeing like a state: How certain schemes to improve the human condition have failed. Yale University Press.

in which they were laid out suited the mechanical *technique* with which they were managed: their navigable laneways provided more easy access for harvest and better matched the zoning and categorization of the tables of data kept in central planning.

But in organizing the forest toward this single-metric view, it had also transformed it. Its *illegible* aspects were reduced or eliminated wherever possible. The countless other uses and products of the forest were being slowly obliterated: *"The monocropped forest was a disaster for peasants who were now deprived of all the grazing, food, raw materials, and medicines that the earlier forest ecology had afforded"*.

These were precisely the aspects that failed to align with the central metric of *"output of timber"*. The utilitarian spruce was planted in place of the previous diverse array of tree species. Fallen trees were cleared. Rotting logs and snags were removed. Every control you can think of was employed to maintain the uniform aesthetic of *legibility*.

It wasn't until almost a hundred years later that these *illegible* factors would lead to the easy discovery of *Waldsterben*. The removal of all other tree species eliminated most animal habitats. The clearing of logs and snags on the forest floor led to a reduction of insects, fungi and bacteria in the already reduced leaf litter. The speed of decomposition slowed, leading to nutrient-poor soils. As the soil compacted from the single species of tree, diversity suffered further, a feedback loop spiraling downward, resulting in further reduction in species diversity.

This was except of course for the singular spruce, which, laid out in their uniform rows, were set like a feast for the previously limited population of insect "pests" (as the planners had defined them). Many of these insects had evolved to specialize alongside the spruce, locked in a complex relationship of competition spanning perhaps a million of years or more. But now the *legible* forest, optimized relentlessly toward its single metric, broke the balance of this ancient struggle, the gates swung open, encouraging plague-like populations of the very "pests" the system had first sought to reduce via its interventions.

The forest was on life support. The system that had once thrived on its own was now entirely dependent on direct human management. It required constant action to keep it alive, with frequent administration of pesticides, fungicides and other external chemicals. Vulnerable and exposed, from there it only took little to destroy the forests entirely, a top-down cascade — a *waldsterben* — to match the top-down legibility that had been imposed upon it.

Seeing the Forest for the Trees

Scott makes the point that the mistake of *legibility* is in trying to impose an idealized vision of order onto a complex, messy reality. In trying to reduce the "*illegible*" we violently dismantle and reduce a system to visually align it with our own goals. Like the planned rows of trees in a plantation, in doing so we lose many of the features that are essential to that system's complex functioning.

The lessons of *legibility* apply to the *Natural Orders* system we've outlined in this book. When it comes to marketing, a skillset like so many others increasingly defined by data and measurement, Scott's idea of *legibility* has daily implications for our decision making. Now more than ever, Scott's ideas can help us avoid the mistakes that so often accompany optimizing metrics and interpreting data.

Throughout the previous chapters, I've attempted to guide you in avoiding the causes of collapse so common to the channel — the top-down and bottom-up cascades of the introductory chapters. I also show you how to build the most profitable strategy possible by focusing first on collecting data; then personalizing offers; then compounding the value of your top customers.

But avoiding the mistakes of *legibility* is also central to *Natural Orders*. The primary objective of marketing is always going to be about increasing the bottom line. But when we become tunnel-visioned about optimizing toward this single metric is when we come unstuck. So rather than imposing an idealized, one-size-fits-all automation solution, I've gone to efforts to ensure that the system we've built is the result of gradual and sustainable growth from strong foundations. I have attempted to guide you in how to best grow an email marketing ecosystem, a Walled Garden, that's safeguarded against our in-built tendency toward shaping it into what appears a more *legible* aesthetic. With *Natural Orders* we've avoided this in several ways.

- As we covered in ***the Walled Gardens***, the competitive practices of the dominant "information empires" places small business owners at a disadvantage. We are exposed to platform risk — the bottom-up cascade — the potential for our audiences to be taken away from us without recourse.

Building an email list solves this problem to a great extent. However, it must be approached with an understanding of why these *Walled Gardens* are so successful in the first place: their competitive advantage depends entirely upon a fervent focus on the customer experience above all else.

The *legible* way to build an email list would be to optimize relentlessly toward improving your website's TSC. This would mean crowding it with intrusive pop-ups or slide-ins, littering your copy with aggressive or dishonest CTAs, or on the other end of the spectrum, reducing the site to little more than a subscription form.

Such single-minded reductionism would have myriad consequences. The overall brand experience would be repulsive for new users. In optimizing only for TSC, we'd destroy the very thing we were working towards: the positive user experience we need in order to be competitive online. Those whom we did manage to coerce into subscribing would likely not be a valuable customer longer term.

The better approach is to temper our subscription CTAs with a focus on value for our site visitors. By setting the standard for the relationship with our subscribers as one based on value, we build a higher quality list and set a stronger foundation for buying behavior later. This approach is continued in our approach in the following chapter.

- In ***Dispersal*** it may have been possible to quickly win sales from new subscribers. But optimizing for sales beyond anything else at this early stage would result in what I termed the *top-down cascade*.

The *legible* way to approach new subscribers would be to email them with a sales pitch immediately after sign-up. Just like the first generation of legible European forests, everything would seem great at first. But over time, the impacts of our interventions would begin to show.

Subscribers would soon tire of the one-sided relationship of your emails. They'll be less likely to interact, and more likely to unsubscribe. The "engagement-retention feedback loop" of our email list would eventually lead to its collapse.

For this reason, we focused instead on always providing *value* to subscribers — to *educate, inspire* and *entertain*. In using the *Five Awareness States* as a guide, the experience of a new subscriber will always be that of value. The entire health of the system is set at a high baseline.

After building the *Awareness Automation*, we also take our first step toward personalizing our email automation strategy for our subscribers. But we also move further into the world of data and measurement, where the tendency toward *legibility* increases further.

- In **Recruitment**, we built a series of automations designed to help reveal the *Black Box* of marketing: defining our customer avatar and the journey they take to purchase. We continued delivering value to our subscribers, while now simultaneously developing them into paying customers.

Consider if we had gone with the *legible* approach in the *Dispersal* stage. In order to maximize conversions, we spam our subscribers with pitches and offers as frequently and as soon after signup as possible. Again, this *legible* optimization toward "increased sales" may have yielded some results in the short term.

But even if we could avoid the top-down cascade of Dispersal, over the medium to long-term our strategy simply wouldn't be able to maximize for the very metric we believed we were optimizing towards. Just as a messy, real-life forest is more "productive" than a planned and managed one, so too would our short-sighted email strategy have been capped in its potential.

It would be predicated on sending offers to a single group of subscribers, with no ability to speak directly to the different segments of our market. With a focus on offers, not value, we'd eventually have an exhausted list of one-time buyers, with no strong relationship with the brand or further interest in what we had to spam them with. Our potential for conversion would be quickly reached.

Instead, the *Recruitment* stage focuses on *personalization* — improving the timing and relevance of the emails we send. We are focused on *learning more* about our market, and in doing so avoid the above outcomes while also providing an experience of value for our individual subscribers. But we don't just provide value, as our timely and relevant messages play to the wants and needs of our segmented audience, producing better conversions. This realization of true maximal outputs is continued in the next chapter:

- In ***Establishment***, we explored how we could make our ecosystem as productive as possible. We built strategies that exploited the distinct pattern in which sales revenue is distributed in our list. By focusing on increasing the AOV and repeat purchases from our top customers, we take the most efficient path to improved revenue.

This again runs contrary to the *legible* path we've traced so far. For many small online business owners, when they think about growing their business the first thing that often comes to mind is to get "more traffic". But this idea is as pervasive as it is misleading. Rarely is it the most direct path.

It is true that improving traffic will increase input to your system. But in practice, maximizing traffic should actually be one of the last steps we take. The system first needs to be optimized so that the traffic we send into it has the greatest likelihood of generating as much revenue as possible.

To this end, the more efficient and profitable way to go about growing your business is actually to focus on your existing customers and improving their LTV. That way, we can first understand and then leverage our improved numbers to access previously prohibitively expensive paid traffic sources.

- Finally, all efforts taken together, we've avoided perhaps the most common of all mistakes in email marketing automation: the attempt to design a masterpiece automation from scratch.

Playing the role of architect, of some *auteur* who will create the masterpiece automation from nothing, is a tempting fantasy. Yet if we've learnt anything from the previous chapters, to do this without feedback is as grandiose as it is unrealistic.

This, as with the other examples, represents the *legible* approach to email marketing automation. With it comes not only the potential for collapse, but the blind optimization toward ideals that may be better achieved with what may seem, at times, as the more lateral approach.

Yet as we've seen, there are natural orders that underlie the structure of your email database. By revealing them and putting them to use, it's possible to cultivate a *Walled Garden* of our own and in turn avoid the risks and competition that defines the current online business environment. Not only do we avoid risks, we actually build an email marketing automation strategy based on the same powerful principles that drive the abundant growth we see in the world that surrounds us every day.

Epicurus in his wisdom was right: we ought to be thankful to nature. Through its lens and its lessons we can more easily discover what's necessary, and filter away what we can safely ignore.

DOWNLOAD FREE RESOURCES

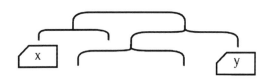

Remember, to access a free tag taxonomy planning document,
as well as the other free resources that come with this book, please visit:
symbiosgrowthautomation.com/natural-orders-resources

REFERENCES

1. Convinceandconvert.com. 13 Email Marketing Statistics That Are Shaping 2019 and Beyond [ONLINE] Available at: https://www.convinceandconvert.com/digital-marketing/email-marketing-statistics/
2. Sendgrid.com. 2019 Email Benchmark and Engagement Study - SendGrid [ONLINE] Available at: https://sendgrid.com/resource/2019-email-benchmark-and-engagement-study/
3. Dma.org.uk. Email's ROI increases, despite concerns about testing and GDPR | DMA [ONLINE] Available at: https://dma.org.uk/press-release/emails-roi-increases-despite-concerns-about-testing-and-gdpr
4. Journal.emergentpublications.com. What can we learn from a theory of complexity? – Emergence: Complexity and Organization [ONLINE] Available at: https://journal.emergentpublications.com/article/what-can-we-learn-from-a-theory-of-complexity/
5. Eolss.net. General Features of Complex Systems [ONLINE] Available at: https://www.eolss.net/Sample-Chapters/C15/E1-29-01-00.pdf
6. Velcro.co.uk. Who Invented VELCRO® Brand Fasteners? | VELCRO® Brand [ONLINE] Available at: https://www.velcro.co.uk/about-us/history/
7. Asknature.org. Versatile Fastener Inspired by Burrs — Innovation — AskNature [ONLINE] Available at: https://asknature.org/innovation/versatile-fastener-inspired-by-burrs/
8. Asknature.org. High Speed Train Inspired by the Kingfisher — Innovation — AskNature [ONLINE] Available at: https://asknature.org/innovation/high-speed-train-inspired-by-the-kingfisher/
9. The Australian, (2020). How the World's Fastest Bird Will Make the Aircraft of the Future [ONLINE] Available at: https://www.theaustralian.com.au/nation/defence/how-worlds-fastest-bird-will-make-aircraft-of-the-future-safer/news-story/24c0b0e43b72c241a518fd30fcbb66a9
10. Howitworksdaily.com. Nature inspired aircraft [ONLINE] Available at: https://www.howitworksdaily.com/the-peregrine-falcon-inspired-aircraft/

11. Asknature.org. Innovation Inspired by Nature — AskNature [ONLINE] Available at: https://asknature.org/
12. Richter, I. A. et al. (2008) Notebooks. Cary, NC: Oxford University Press.
13. Sutherland, R. (2019) Alchemy: The dark art and curious science of creating magic in brands, business, and life. New York, NY: HarperAudio.
14. Clements, F. (1916) "Plant Succession: An Analysis of the Development of Vegetation," Carnegie Institution of Washington, 242.
15. Eugenewei.com. "Platform" risk — Remains of the Day [ONLINE] Available at: https://www.eugenewei.com/blog/2015/3/14/platform-risk
16. Stevefaktor.com. The Risk that Ate the Digital Entrepreneur - Surviving Platform Risk [ONLINE] Available at: https://stevefaktor.com/platform-risk-devours-digital-entrepreneurs/
17. Druriley.com. Platform Risk - Dru Riley [ONLINE] Available at: https://druriley.com/platform-risk/
18. Blog.simeonov.com. Startup anti-pattern: platform risk | HighContrast [ONLINE] Available at: https://blog.simeonov.com/2013/03/05/platform-risk-anti-pattern/
19. Observer.com. Broken on Purpose: Why Getting It Wrong Pays More Than Getting It Right | Observer [ONLINE] Available at: https://observer.com/2012/09/broken-on-purpose/
20. Jason Sadler. It's Not Cool That Facebook Wants Me to Pay To Reach My Fans With Promoted Posts - WSJ [ONLINE] Available at: https://www.wsj.com/articles/SB10001424052702303740704577521072755665762
21. Mathew Ingram. Remember, Facebook isn't a platform for you to use - you are a platform for Facebook to use - Gigaom [ONLINE] Available at: https://gigaom.com/2013/03/04/remember-facebook-isnt-a-platform-for-you-to-use-you-are-a-platform-for-facebook-to-use/
22. Pymnts.com. Amazon, Walmart Nearly Tied In Share Of Retail | PYMNTS.com [ONLINE] Available at: https://www.pymnts.com/news/retail/2021/amazon-walmart-nearly-tied-in-full-year-share-of-retail-sales/
23. Dana Mattioli. How Amazon Wins: By Steamrolling Rivals and Partners - WSJ [ONLINE] Available at: https://www.wsj.com/articles/amazon-competition-shopify-wayfair-allbirds-antitrust-11608235127

24. Fortune.com. Amazon's Jeff Bezos: The Ultimate Disrupter | Fortune [ONLINE] Available at: https://fortune.com/2012/11/16/amazons-jeff-bezos-the-ultimate-disrupter/
25. Ec.europa.eu. Antitrust: EC opens formal investigation against Amazon [ONLINE] Available at: https://ec.europa.eu/commission/presscorner/detail/pl/ip_19_4291
26. Dana Mattioli, Patience Haggin and Shane Shifflett. Amazon Restricts How Rival Device Makers Buy Ads on Its Site - WSJ [ONLINE] Available at: https://www.wsj.com/articles/amazon-restricts-advertising-competitor-device-makers-roku-arlo-11600786638?mod=article_inline
27. Examine.com. Why has Examine.com disappeared from search results? | Examine.com [ONLINE] Available at: https://examine.com/nutrition/google-update-july-2019/
28. Techcrunch.com. Google In Discussions To Acquire Yelp For A Half Billion Dollars Or More | TechCrunch [ONLINE] Available at: https://techcrunch.com/2009/12/17/google-acquire-buy-yelp/
29. Businessinsider.com. Google Wants to Kill Yelp [ONLINE] Available at: https://www.businessinsider.com/google-wants-to-kill-yelp-2012-12?IR=T
30. Seekingalpha.com. Programmatic Advertising: Walled Gardens May Be The Real Winners | Seeking Alpha [ONLINE] Available at: https://seekingalpha.com/article/4332959-programmatic-advertising-walled-gardens-may-be-real-winners
31. Warc.com. Walled gardens are the future for brands | WARC [ONLINE] Available at: https://www.warc.com/newsandopinion/news/walled-gardens-are-the-future-for-brands/42981
32. Tech-bytes.net. Walled gardens are growing taller: Platform lock-in — Tech Bytes - Articles - Tech Bytes [ONLINE] Available at: https://tech-bytes.net/posts/2017/10/9/walled-gardens-are-growing-taller
33. Sachin Kamdar. 3 Things About Walled Gardens That Drive Digital Publishers 'Up The Wall' [ONLINE] Available at: https://www.forbes.com/sites/sachinkamdar/2015/10/18/3-things-about-walled-gardens-that-drive-digital-publishers-up-the-wall/?sh=224d9d634aae
34. Finance.yahoo.com. Should News Sites Make a 'Faustian Bargain' With Facebook? [ONLINE] Available at: https://finance.yahoo.com/news/should-news-sites-make-a-faustian-bargain-with-114596098814.html?guccounter=1

35. Npr.org. Airbnb: Joe Gebbia : How I Built This with Guy Raz : NPR [ONLINE] Available at: https://www.npr.org/2017/10/19/543035808/airbnb-joe-gebbia
36. McLuhan, M. (1969) The Gutenberg Galaxy. Signet Book.
37. Hughes, R. (1991) The shock of the new: Art and the century of change. London, England: Thames & Hudson.
38. Barrett, W. (1979) Illusion of Technique. Glasgow, Scotland: HarperCollins Distribution Services.
39. Ellul, J. (1973) The Technological Society. New York, NY: Random House.
40. Voltaire (1968) Candide. Edited by J. H. Brumfitt. London, England: Oxford University Press.
41. Usv.com. Fat Protocols | Union Square Ventures [ONLINE] Available at: https://www.usv.com/writing/2016/08/fat-protocols/
42. Growrevenue.io. What's a good bounce rate? (Here's the average bounce rate for websites) - GrowRevenue.io [ONLINE] Available at: https://growrevenue.io/bounce-rate-benchmarks/
43. Sumo Group, Inc.. Email Signup Benchmarks: How Many Visitors Should Be Converting [ONLINE] Available at: https://sumo.com/stories/email-signup-benchmarks
44. Nateliason.com. I'm killing most of my email capture. Here's why. - Nat Eliason [ONLINE] Available at: https://www.nateliason.com/blog/email-capture
45. Mutinyfund.com. The Mutiny Tail Risk Fund - A Long Volatility Investment Approach [ONLINE] Available at: https://mutinyfund.com/
46. Watson & Wolfe. Journal - Listen, Watch & Read Articles to Entertain & Inspire | Watson & Wolfe – Watson & Wolfe [ONLINE] Available at: https://www.watsonwolfe.com/the-journal-blog/
47. Taylorpearson.me. Improve Your Decision-Making Using an Expected Value Calculator [ONLINE] Available at: https://taylorpearson.me/expected-value-calculator/
48. Vox.com. BuzzFeed's founder used to write Marxist theory and it explains BuzzFeed perfectly - Vox [ONLINE] Available at: https://www.vox.com/2014/5/20/5730762/buzzfeeds-founder-used-to-write-marxist-theory-and-it-explains
49. Tryinteract.com. How to Design an Email Opt-in Form That Converts at 50% | Interact Blog [ONLINE] Available at: https://www.tryinteract.com/blog/how-to-design-an-email-opt-in-form-that-converts-at-50/

50. Couponscience.org. 2019 Coupon and Promo Code Use Study | OHC [ONLINE] Available at: https://couponscience.org/iherb/2017-coupon-promo-code-study/
51. Andrewchen.com. The Law of Shitty Clickthroughs at andrewchen [ONLINE] Available at: https://andrewchen.com/the-law-of-shitty-clickthroughs/
52. Michael J. Vardon and Christopher R. Tidemann (2000) "The black flying-fox (Pteropus alecto) in north Australia: juvenile mortality and longevity," Australian Journal of Zoology, 48, pp. 91–97.
53. Serc.carleton.edu. Introduction to Complex Systems [ONLINE] Available at: https://serc.carleton.edu/NAGTWorkshops/complexsystems/introduction.html#feedback
54. Expandedramblings.com. 90 Interesting Facts About Email | How Many Emails are Sent Per Day? [ONLINE] Available at: https://expandedramblings.com/index.php/email-statistics/
55. Schwartz, E. M. (2017) Breakthrough advertising: How to write ads that shatter traditions and sales records. Book on Demand.
56. Collier, R. (2016) The Robert Collier letter book. North Charleston, SC: Createspace Independent Publishing Platform.
57. Newell, A. and Simon, H. A. (1971) Human Problem Solving. Harlow, England: Longman Higher Education.
58. Stratechery.com. Defining Aggregators – Stratechery by Ben Thompson [ONLINE] Available at: https://stratechery.com/2017/defining-aggregators/
59. Pearson, T. (2015) The end of jobs: Money, meaning and freedom without the 9-to-5. Three Magnolia.
60. Gleick, J. (2011) The information: A history, a theory, a flood. New York, NY: Pantheon Books.
61. Pwc.com. Data the new Smart [ONLINE] Available at: https://www.pwc.com/ng/en/assets/pdf/data-the-new-smart.pdf
62. Bernardmarr.com. How Much Data Is There In the World? | Bernard Marr [ONLINE] Available at: https://bernardmarr.com/how-much-data-is-there-in-the-world/
63. Peter Lyman, Hal R. Varian, et al (2000) "How Much Information?" Available at: https://groups.ischool.berkeley.edu/archive/how-much-info/how-much-info.pdf.

References

64. Theverge.com. Google's parent company briefly hits $2 trillion valuation - The Verge [ONLINE] Available at: https://www.theverge.com/2021/11/8/22770569/alphabet-google-market-cap-hits-2-trillion
65. Eyal, N. (2014) Hooked: How to build habit-forming products. London, England: Portfolio Penguin.
66. MarketingSherpa. Welcome Messages Get Highest Open Rates of All Email Campaigns: How to Improve Yours | MarketingSherpa [ONLINE] Available at: https://www.marketingsherpa.com/article/how-to/how-to-improve-yours
67. Createandsell.co. Yesterday, Apple obliterated email open tracking - Create & Sell [ONLINE] Available at: https://createandsell.co/issues/apple-block-open-tracking
68. Apple.com. Apple advances its privacy leadership with iOS 15, iPadOS 15, macOS Monterey, and watchOS 8 - Apple [ONLINE] Available at: https://www.apple.com/newsroom/2021/06/apple-advances-its-privacy-leadership-with-ios-15-ipados-15-macos-monterey-and-watchos-8/
69. Gon.to. You're Measuring Your Email Nurtures Effectiveness Wrong [ONLINE] Available at: https://gon.to/2017/01/25/you-re-measuring-your-email-nurtures-effectiveness-wrong/
70. Dennis J. O'Dowd and A. Malcolm Gill (0108/1984) "Predator Satiation and Site Alteration Following Fire: Mass Reproduction of Alpine Ash (Eucalyptus Delegatensis) in Southeastern Australia," Ecology, 65(4), pp. 1052–1066.
71. Mittelbach, G. G. and McGill, B. J. (2019) Community Ecology. 2nd ed. London, England: Oxford University Press.
72. Kotler, P. (1991) Marketing Management: Analysis, Planning, Implementation and Control. 7th ed. London, England: Prentice-Hall.
73. Barilliance.com, (2021). Complete List of Cart Abandonment Rate Statistics: 2006-2021 [ONLINE] Available at: https://www.barilliance.com/cart-abandonment-rate-statistics/#tab-con-7
74. Barilliance.com, (2021). 2021 Email Marketing ROI Statistics: Open Rate to Revenue [ONLINE] Available at: https://www.barilliance.com/email-marketing-statistics/
75. Sightseeingtoursaustralia.com.au. Why is the Daintree Rainforest Important? [ONLINE] Available at: https://sightseeingtoursaustralia.com.au/tips-articles/why-is-the-daintree-rainforest-important/

76. Australiangeographic.com.au. The Idiot Fruit Tree - Australian Geographic [ONLINE] Available at: https://www.australiangeographic.com.au/topics/science-environment/2017/07/the-idiot-fruit-tree/
77. Wettropics.gov.au. Butterflyfacts [ONLINE] Available at: https://www.wettropics.gov.au/site/user-assets/docs/butterflyfacts.pdf
78. Youtube.com. Sir David Attenborough Endorses Tropical North Queensland - YouTube [ONLINE] Available at: https://www.youtube.com/watch?v=_EdXkEImSps&list=PL2fcnDR1IIEtzlPhQ1q_NSPTlwC7E21lW&index=6
79. Wet Tropics Management Authority. World Heritage Area - facts and figures | Wet Tropics Management Authority [ONLINE] Available at: https://www.wettropics.gov.au/world-heritage-area-facts-and-figures.html
80. Diamond, J. M. (1997) Guns, germs and steel: The fates of human societies. London, England: Jonathan Cape.
81. Dailytelegraph.com.au. Australian Reptile Park keepers step in with riot shields during attempt to mate cassowaries | Daily Telegraph [ONLINE] Available at: https://www.dailytelegraph.com.au/newslocal/central-coast/australian-reptile-park-keepers-step-in-with-riot-shields-during-attempt-to-mate-cassowaries/news-story/7ae804e2f417c6372b927ecaf67b495f
82. Wet Tropics Management Authority. Cassowaries | Wet Tropics Management Authority [ONLINE] Available at: https://www.wettropics.gov.au/cassowaries
83. Si.edu. Numbers of Insects (Species and Individuals) | Smithsonian Institution [ONLINE] Available at: https://www.si.edu/spotlight/buginfo/bugnos
84. IISC (2011) "State of Observed Species," National Institute for Species Exploration. Available at: https://www.esf.edu/species/documents/sos2011.pdf.
85. Cooper, L., Kang, S.Y., Bisanzio, D. et al. (2019) "Pareto rules for malaria super-spreaders and super-spreading," Nat Commun, 10(3939).
86. Livescience.com. Facts About Rainforests | Live Science [ONLINE] Available at: https://www.livescience.com/63196-rainforest-facts.html
87. Fred J. Rispoli and Suhua Zeng et al (2014) "Even birds follow Pareto's 80–20 rule," Significance (Oxford, England), 11(1), pp. 37–38.

88. Livescience.com. A Few Tree Species Dominate Amazon Rain Forest | Live Science [ONLINE] Available at: https://www.livescience.com/40508-few-tree-species-dominate-amazon-rainforest.html
89. R.R. van der Ploeg, W. Böhm, M.B. Kirkham, (1999), On the origin of the theory of mineral nutrition of plants and the law of the minimum, Soil Science Society of America Journal 63, 1055–1062.
90. Hbr.org. The Value of Keeping the Right Customers [ONLINE] Available at: https://hbr.org/2014/10/the-value-of-keeping-the-right-customers
91. Thompson, D. W. (1942) On Growth and Form. Cambridge, England: Cambridge University Press.
92. Komulainen, T. (no date) "Self-Similarity and Power Laws," Helsinki University of Technology Laboratory of Process Control and Automation. Available at: http://neocybernetics.com/report145/Chapter10.pdf.
93. Crazyegg.com. How to Profit from Upsells, Cross-Sells and Bundles [ONLINE] Available at: https://www.crazyegg.com/blog/upsells-cross-sells-bundle-sells/
94. The-future-of-commerce.com. E-commerce cross-sell and up-sell: The difference, benefits, and examples [ONLINE] Available at: https://www.the-future-of-commerce.com/2013/10/14/ecommerce-cross-sell-up-sell/
95. Mckinsey.com. How retailers can keep up with consumers | McKinsey [ONLINE] Available at: https://www.mckinsey.com/industries/retail/our-insights/how-retailers-can-keep-up-with-consumers
96. Smartinsights.com. E-commerce conversion rates benchmarks 2022 - How do yours compare? [ONLINE] Available at: https://www.smartinsights.com/ecommerce/ecommerce-analytics/ecommerce-conversion-rates/
97. Business.adobe.com. Adobe Digital Economy Index | Adobe Analytics [ONLINE] Available at: https://business.adobe.com/ca/resources/digital-economy-index.html
98. Media.bain.com. The Value of Online Customer Loyalty and How You Can Capture It [ONLINE] Available at: https://media.bain.com/Images/Value_online_customer_loyalty_you_capture.pdf
99. Hbr.org. The Value of Keeping the Right Customers [ONLINE] Available at: https://hbr.org/2014/10/the-value-of-keeping-the-right-customers

100. Chris Best. A better future for news [ONLINE] Available at: https://on.substack.com/p/a-better-future-for-news
101. Backlinko.com. Substack User and Revenue Statistics (2022) [ONLINE] Available at: https://backlinko.com/substack-users
102. Nathan Pettijohn. Why Every Company Is A Media Company [ONLINE] Available at: https://www.forbes.com/sites/nathanpettijohn/2019/02/07/why-every-company-is-a-media-company/?sh=269d283b7391
103. Shopify.com. Ecommerce Loyalty Programs: 25 Strategies from 100+ Results & Stats [ONLINE] Available at: https://www.shopify.com/enterprise/ecommerce-loyalty-programs#1
104. Rubygarage.org. Everything You Should Know About Ecommerce Loyalty Programs [ONLINE] Available at: https://rubygarage.org/blog/guide-to-online-loyalty-programs
105. Bigcommerce.com. Ecommerce Loyalty Programs: Reward Customers + Drive Sales (2021) [ONLINE] Available at: https://www.bigcommerce.com/blog/online-customer-loyalty-programs/#types-of-customer-loyalty-programs
106. Scott, J. C. (1999) Seeing like a state: How certain schemes to improve the human condition have failed. Yale University Press.

ACKNOWLEDGEMENTS

Thanks to everyone who provided formative feedback on (very) rough first drafts, especially Taylor Pearson and members of the DC writing group: Viola Eva, Ethan Drower, Rayru Fonseca and Harvey Hancock.

Thanks to all the early readers who took time to provide crucial feedback for various other versions that followed: Leon van Kammen, Teddy Smith, Kate Hill, Bola Marquis, Stephen Tasker, Peter Murphy Lewis, Alex McQuade, Chris Bourgalt, Evan Demkiw, Jed Tabaczynski, Eyram Adjogatse, Steve Lauman, Foster Hodge, Judy Schramm, Nir Eyal and Julie Li Eyal.

Paula, Mum, and Dad —for your love and support.

*... to the eyes of the man of imagination,
nature is imagination itself*

William Blake

Printed in Poland
by Amazon Fulfillment
Poland Sp. z o.o., Wrocław